STUDIES IN
FEMINISM

STUDIES IN
FEMINISM

Edited by

Lilack Biswas

Assistant Professor
Department of English
Dinabandhu Mahavidyalaya
Bongaon, North 24 Parganas
West Bengal, India

PARTRIDGE

To order additional copies of this book, contact
Partridge India
000 800 10062 62
orders.india@partridgepublishing.com

www.partridgepublishing.com/india

Contents

Dedicated to the Lotus Feet of Mahatma Shri Narayan Goswami for being the Friend Philosopher and Guide and showering his limitless bliss on such an inferior soul like me.

Introduction

It is universally known that Modern Feminism, like many other social and political movements, originated as a movement for the equal right of women in all social political and economic spheres. To some extent it seems to me that modern feminism was born in the womb of Marxism and nourished in the lap of existentialism, particularly in the writing of Simone de Beauvoir. The Marxist notion of class division of the *haves* and the *have nots* gave a sense to the feminist thinkers that women in the male dominated society were actually a class similar to the *have nots* who actually lived for the males not for their own. A sense of insecurity …. A sense of non-being …. Simone de Beauvoir hit this point and associated the crisis with Jean Paul Sartre's precept of "existence precedes essence" and proclaimed that "one is not born a woman, but becomes one." The spirit of female liberty and quest for equal right did not restrict itself into the strict delimitations of political or social arena. It got sufficient popularity and exposure in arts, literature and films in the coming decades. Historians Maggie Humm and Rebecca Walker have divided the history of modern feminist movements into three parts calling them "waves". The first wave starts in the late nineteenth and early twentieth century, the second wave in the nineteen sixties and seventies and the third wave in the nineteen nineties and lasts to the present. The feminist thinkers before these waves have been called "proto feminists" by some critics while some others have objected this nomenclature.

In the present meaning of the term, feminism does not only mean a woman's struggle for equal right or social, political or economic empowerment. Now- a -days feminism means much more. It includes typical feminine experiences, like puberty, menstruation, pregnancy, child birth, rape, molestation etc. the intellectual and emotional subordinations by patriarchal social forces. If we accept this notion of Feminism we cannot limit its scope only in modern age, only within the so called "waves". There are thousands of examples of strong feminist notions even in ancient literatures of both orient and occident.

In The Iliad we can see a number of female characters who do not give in to the patriarchal impositions and try to raise their voices. One such character is Clytemnestra who had the guts to protest her husband against the sacrifice of her daughter. She actually raised her voice against the established social norms, and presented a woman's demand (not of a queen's) when she insisted her husband King Agamemnon not to go for the Trojan war, which was turned down by the former and resulted into an adulterous relation of the earlier with Aegisthus. It is also noteworthy that in those days she dared to involve in an extramarital relationship which ultimately resulted the assassination of Agamemnon. In the Ramayana or The Mahabharata also we can find some characters that make themselves different with their indomitable spirit and demand of respect. The point behind these citations is the objection against the phrase "proto feminist". It is impossible to label any poet or writer of the ancient age as a proto feminist though they have show strong notions of women liberty and the demands of women. This introduction is a very short place to discuss these matters elaborately.

A century old and widely used tool of women subordination is Religion. Religion plays a vital role in the shaping of a society. From ancient to present day religious forces are undeniable. The lives of women in the society have always been a thing of special importance to each and every religion and the so called religious people. Therefore when a woman raises her voice for the demand of respect, right, education, privacy, marriage, sexual preference etc, it sometimes goes against the set religious beliefs and the woman has to fight not only against patriarchy but also its counterpart religion. The article written by Dr. Bittoo Rani throws ample light on the religious views. What the original scriptures say and what the patriarchal voices impose upon and how it adulterates the religious doctrines to make it a weapon of injustice.

In this present collection of essays and articles on various issues of feminine interest a deliberate effort has been given to maintain its range. Here we get feminist interpretations of the ancient characters like Sita or Madri as well as the sexually unsatisfied woman in Alifa Rifaat's story. From the princess and queens to the next door girl, the grand and the plebian; all are placed on the equal plane in terms of their pains, sufferings and sacrifices of being women.

I extend my cordial thanks to all the contributors for enriching this collection with their clarity of thought and accuracy of expression combined with depth of research.

Lilack Biswas

Chapter 1

Bridging the Gender Gaps through Women Empowerment: A Linchpin for Sustainable Development of India

RATAN SARKAR
Research Scholar
Ramakrishna Mission Vivekananda University,
Faculty of Disability Management
and Special Education,
Coimbatore, Tamil Nadu

INTRODUCTION

Gender discrimination continues to be an enormous problem within Indian society. Traditional patriarchal norms have relegated women to secondary status within the household and workplace. This drastically affects women's health, financial status, education, and political involvement. Women are commonly married young, quickly become mothers, and are then burdened by stringent domestic and financial responsibilities. They are frequently malnourished since women typically are the last member of a household to eat and the last to receive medical attention. Additionally, there is a wide gender disparity in the literacy rate in India: effective literacy rates (age 7 and above) in 2011 were 82.14% for men and only 65.46% for women (United Nations Population Fund, 2009). Women receive little schooling, and suffer from unfair and biased inheritance and divorce laws. These laws prevent women from accumulating substantial financial assets, making it difficult for women to establish their own security and autonomy. Women are usually left behind to care and provide for the entire household. Women are not provided equal wages even thought they are in a position like men. This custom leaves little opportunity for the growth and development of women's rights and education levels. In India, from time immemorial, a girl child has been considered as an unwanted entity and a burden that the parents would not mind doing away with. Discrimination against women begins even before her birth. The gruesome evils of female feticide and infanticide prove how brutal the world could be to women. Though the Indian constitution provides equal rights and privileges for men and women and makes equal provision to improve the status of women in society, majority of women are still unable to enjoy the rights and opportunities guaranteed to them. Traditional value system, low level of literacy, more house hold responsibilities lack of awareness, non-availability of proper guidance, low mobility, lack of self confidence family discouragement, poverty, unemployment, and anti-female attitude are some of the factors responsible to create gender disparity in Indian society.

However the promotion of gender equality and empowering of women is one of the eight Millennium Development Goals (MDG) to which India is a signatory. Gender equality is a goal in its own right but also a key factor for sustainable economic growth, social development and environmental sustainability. Research study (Lidia Farre, 2012) reveals that women's contribution in social progress is more important than that of men. Women have also been rightly recognized for their role in supporting movements for democracy, human rights and peace. Their contribution to sustainable development is equally significant. Study after study has demonstrated that women are pivotal to addressing hunger, malnutrition and poverty. They are the farmers and nurturers, the entrepreneurs and educators, the healers and helpers who can contribute to food security and economic growth in the country's most remote and vulnerable settings. Despite the heavy responsibility women shoulder, they lack equal access to opportunities and resources. This hampers their advancement and holds all people back. Studies reveal that more than 100 million people could be lifted out of poverty if women had the same access to productive resources as men. Productivity in farms could be increased up to 30 percent with the active participation of women. The number of hungry people would drop by as much as 17 per cent - an impact that translates into improvements for as many as 150 million individuals (Food and Agriculture Organization of the United Nations, Rome, 2011). The benefits would reverberate even further as these women's children gain better access to health services, education and nutrition. In the developing country like India the gross domestic product would increase by up to 2%-4% annually, if women's employment rates were raised to 70% from 30% at present (UNESCAP-2007, Economic and Social Survey of Asia and the Pacific).

However, now question arises what is the way out to achieve these gains removing the gender gaps? The answer is obvious; it is only through the empowerment of women. Women empowerment can be achieved by investing in women, eliminating any forms of discriminations against them in law and in practice, ensuring that policy respond to their needs, giving equal opportunity to access to resources, and providing disadvantaged women with a role in decision-making. These measures will in turn help drive sustainable development - one of the great imperatives of the twenty first century.

WOMEN EMPOWERMENT

The term 'Empowerment' can also be defined as a "multi-dimensional social process that helps people gain control over their own lives. It is a process that fosters power (that is, the capacity to implement) in people, for use in their own lives, their communities, and in their society, by acting on issues that they define as important" (Page and Czuba, 1999). However, women empowerment is the process of empowering the women to take their own decisions for their personal dependent and make them independent in all aspects from mind, thought, rights, decisions, etc by leaving all the social and family limitations. It is to bring equality in the society for both male and female in all areas. According to the United Nations Population Fund an empowered woman has a sense of self worth. She can determine her own choices, and has access to opportunities and resources providing her with an array of options she can pursue. She has control over her own life, both within and outside the home and she has the ability to influence the direction of social change to create a more just social and economic order, both nationally and internationally (UNDP, 2008). Women empowerment is very necessary to make the bright future of the family, society and country. This fundamental truth was also revealed when Pandit Jawaharlal Nehru (1889 -1964) stated that: "To awaken the people, it is the women who must be awakened. Once she is on the move, the family moves, the village moves, the nation moves". Women need fresh and more capable environment so that they can take their own right decisions in every area whether for themselves, family, society or country. The discussion about women's empowerment in this paper is held against the backdrop of women's continued disadvantage compared to men. This disadvantage is apparent in the different spheres of personal, economic, socio-cultural and political life in all the societies in India. Empowerment in this context means women gaining more power and control over their own lives. As such, it can be conceptualized as an important process in reaching gender equality.

GENDER EQUALITY

Gender equality is understood to mean that the "rights, responsibilities and opportunities of individuals will not depend on whether they are born male or female". What is expected of a man or a woman, a girl or a boy, differs depending on the socio-cultural context in which they live. Gender roles are learnt by each person through socialization processes. In other words: what he or she learns from others through the social interactions they have with their families, peers and society at large. This means that gender roles and gender role expectations are not fixed and can change over time in the same way that they differ across different societies. On a larger scale, gender role expectations are institutionalized through legislation, education, political and economic systems, culture and traditions. These institutions structure social and cultural life and create gendered norms and practices. The gendered division of labour in everyday life is an example: women continue to play a dominant role in providing unpaid care to family members and taking care of domestic chores but they play a subordinate role in political and economic life. As women dedicate more time to unpaid activities, they are often dependent on men's income and less protected through financial savings, pension, entitlements and property in their name. This means that women are at greater risk of poverty and have fewer opportunities in the labour market. Therefore, the general understanding is that women need to be "empowered" in order to narrow the "gender gap" and this in turn reveals that gender equality and women empowerment are two sides of the same coin: progress toward gender equality requires women's empowerment and women's empowerment requires increases in gender equality.

SUSTAINABLE DEVELOPMENT

In the late 1980s the report 'Our Common Future' by the 'World Commission on Environment and Development' defined the concept "Sustainable Development" as development which "meets the needs of the present without compromising the ability of future generations to meet their own needs". While aiming to maximize the well-being of today's generation, it is important to take a long-term perspective, taking into account the consequences of our actions for our children, their children and grandchildren, ensuring that the resources they will require for their own well-being are not depleted, and that the natural environment into which they will be born will not be destroyed. Sustainable development is conceptualized as resting on three inter-related pillars: economic development, social development and environmental protection. A fourth pillar-the preservation of cultural diversity has been proposed. This conceptual categorization can lead to treating these areas in isolation without accounting for a whole range of channels through which these pillars reinforce each other and bring about sustainable development. Instead, by taking an integrated and holistic approach to socio-culturally responsible, environmentally-friendly economic development, sustainable development can be revealed as a multifaceted and dynamic process. It is also revealed that "the goal, and indeed the ultimate test, of sustainable development is the convergence among the three trajectories of economic growth, social development and environmental protection". In this spirit it is important to acknowledge that the promotion of gender equality also requires a cross-cutting and integrative approach. It is important not to conceptualize women's empowerment and gender equality as a question of social development alone, but as a cross-cutting issue in economic and socio-cultural development and environmental protection.

VARIOUS WAYS OF WOMEN EMPOWERMENT

The following ways can be undertaken for ensuring gender equality and women empowerment:

1. **Promoting Leadership quality:**

   - Affirm high-level support and direct top-level policies for gender equality and human rights.
   - Engage women in the development process of policies, schemes, programmes and implementation plans at all levels.
   - Ensure that all policies are gender sensitive - identifying factors that impact women and men differently- and incorporate culture advances equality and inclusion.

2. **Provide Equal Opportunity, Ensure Complete Inclusion and Non-discrimination:**

   - Pay equal remuneration, including benefits, for work of equal value and strive to pay a living wage to all women and men.
   - Ensure that workplace policies and practices are free from gender-based discrimination.
   - Implement gender-sensitive recruitment and retention practices and proactively recruit and appoint women to administrative, managerial and executive positions.
   - Assure sufficient participation of women - 30% or greater - in decision-making and governance at all levels.

- Offer flexible employment options, leave and re-entry opportunities to positions of equal pay and status.
- Support access to child and dependent care by providing services, resources and information to both women and men.

3. **Ensuring Health, Safety and Freedom from Violence:**

- Taking into account differential impacts on women and men, provide safe working conditions and protection from exposure to hazardous materials and disclose potential risks, including to reproductive health.
- Establish a zero-tolerance policy towards all forms of violence at work, including verbal and/or physical abuse, and prevent sexual harassment.
- Strive to offer health insurance or other needed services - including for survivors of domestic violence - and ensure equal access for all legal actions.
- Respect women and men workers' rights to time off for medical care and counseling for themselves and their dependents.
- Taking initiatives for providing legal supports to the women for any forms of violence under any circumstances.
- Train security staff and managers to recognize signs of violence against women and understand laws and company policies on human trafficking, labour and sexual exploitation.

4. **Education and Training:**

- Invest more in women education. This is the most important investment which in turn will promote gender equality and women empowerment leading to sustainable development.
- Ensure equal access to education and training programmes, including literacy classes, vocational and information technology training.
- Provide equal opportunities for formal and informal education and training.
- Offer equal opportunities to both male and female for vocational education and training programme in order to ensure equal and gainful employment.

5. **Agriculture and Enterprise Development, Supply Chain and Marketing Practices:**

- Give training to rural women to take part in the agricultural activities actively.
- Expand small businesses, and women entrepreneurs.
- Support gender-sensitive solutions to credit and lending barriers.
- Ask business partners and peers to respect the company's commitment to advancing equality and inclusion.
- Respect the dignity of women in all marketing and other company materials.
- Ensure that company products, services and facilities are not used for human trafficking and/or labour or sexual exploitation.

WOMEN EMPOWERMENT AND SUSTAINABLE DEVELOPMENT: INTER-DEPENDENCE AND INTER-RELATION

Sustainable development depends on the allocation of resources between women and men, on the one hand, and, on the other, by how these resources are spread over time and generations. One objective of sustainable development is to satisfy the needs of the present. It calls for a more equitable distribution of resources among those living today where resources are unequally distributed. At the same time sustainable development requires a strategic perspective to account for what women and men are leaving for the next generation. However, presently income is unequally distributed between women and men. As women take on the primary responsibility for the unpaid care of children and the elderly and for unpaid domestic labour, fewer women than men are in paid employment. Due to the discrepancy in earnings, women accumulate less income than men over their lifetime. Their lower earnings increase their vulnerability to poverty, not only during their working lives but also in old age, and increase their economic dependence on a male breadwinner. This income gap reduces their opportunities to set up their own businesses to gain economic independence. Many working women, in addition to being financially disadvantaged compared to men, also bear the effects of "time poverty" as responsibilities in the home and family life are unequally shared. Women's advocacy groups have drawn attention to the important role that women are playing as natural resource managers and agents of change. However, it is important to recognize this role and to draw on women's commitment and expertise in shaping strategies and decisions. This not only refers to the important challenges faced with regard to protecting our natural environment. It also refers to the question of state debts which are accumulating and are being passed on to future generations; it refers to the responsibility of creating sustainable social protection systems in the ageing societies of our region. Women's contribution to sustainable development, and their knowledge and skills, must be recognized. Women have a strong role in educating and socializing their children, including teaching them care and responsibility with regard to the use and protection of natural resources. Today, women are still underrepresented among those who take the decisions that will impact future generations. Under these circumstances questions arises what can be done to solve this gender disparity? The answer is- a gender-sensitive approach must be introduced in order to bring gender equality and ensure sustainable development. Sustainable development cannot be achieved without a more equitable distribution of resources today and tomorrow: prevailing inequalities are deeply gendered. Understanding this and acting upon it is a key condition to achieving sustainable development. Taking women's needs, concerns and their knowledge and skills into account will ensure a better understanding of the dynamics in society which create and perpetuate gender inequality and enable policymakers and other agents of change, including employers and civil society organizations, to develop appropriate policy responses and actions. Equal participation in decision-making and a balanced involvement of both men and women at all levels of implementation will ensure that women and men take equal responsibility for today's and future generations.

CONCLUSION

To conclude it can be stated that women empowerment and gender equality are interchangeable terms. One cannot be achieved without another. These two terms are also used as inter-related and inter-dependent terms in sustainable development goal which requires action on three fronts: social, economic and environmental. Women are central to progress in each area which makes commitments to ensuring women's equal rights and opportunities. This requires empowering women and dropping discriminatory barriers in diverse areas, among them agriculture, energy, health, education, employment and disaster risk reduction.

REFERENCES

1. Farre, L. (2012). The role of men in the economic and social development of women - implications for gender equality. Retrieved from: http://www.iae.csic.es/investigatorsMaterial/a1257115127archivoPdf85747.pdf, on 25.08.2015.

2. Ganesamurthy, V.S. (2008). Empowerment of women in India: Social, Economic and Political. New Delhi: New Century Publications.

3. Page, N. & Czuba, C. E. (1999). Empowerment: What Is It? Journal of Extension, *Volume No. 37, Issue- 5.* Retrieved from: http://www.joe.org/joe/1999october/comm1.php, on 31.08.2015.

4. Rao, M. K. (2005). Empowerment of Women in India. New Delhi: Discovering Publishing House.

5. Rao, M.K. (2005). Women Empowerment in India. New Delhi: Discovery Publishing House.

6. Tarique, Md. & S, Sana. (2013). Education, Equality and Women Empowerment: An Analysis. The International Journal of Entrepreneurship and Business Environment Perspective (IJEBEP); Volume No. 2, Issue No. 2, ISSN: 2279-0918, Pp-379-387.

7. The State of Food and Agriculture. (2011). Women in Agriculture Closing the gender gap for development Rome: Food and Agriculture Organization of the United Nations. Retrieved from: http://www.fao.org/docrep/013/i2050e/i2050e.pdf, on 02.08.2015.

8. UNDP. (2008). Innovative Approaches to Women's Economic Empowerment. Retrieved from: http://content.undp.org/go/cms-service/stream/asset/?asset_id=2524504, on 02.2015

9. UNECE. (2009). Gender Equality, Work and Old Age. UNECE Policy Brief on Ageing. Retrieved from: http://www.unece.org/pau/_docs/age/2009/Policy_briefs/2, on 02.09.2015.

10. UNECE. (2009). Measuring Sustainable Development (ECE/CES/77). Retrieved from: http://www.unece.org/stats/publications/Measuring_sustainable_development.pdf.on 03.09.2015.

11. UNECE. (2010). The MDGs in Europe and Central Asia: Achievements, Challenges and the Way Forward (ECE/INF/2010/2). Retrieved from: http://www.unece.org/commission/MDGs/2010_MDG.pdf, on 03.09.2015.

12. UNESCAP. (2007). Economic and Social Survey of Asia and the Pacific. Retrieved from: http://www.unescap.org/resources/economic-and-social-survey-asia-and-pacific-2007, on 23.08.2015.

13. UNFPA. (2009).State of World Population 2009; Facing a Changing World: Women, Population and Climate. Retrieved from: https://www.unfpa.org/sites/default/files/pub-pdf/state_of_world_population_2009.pdf, 12.08.2015.

14. Warth, L. & Koparanova, M. (2012). Empowering Women for Sustainable Development. Geneva: United Nations Economic Commission for Europe.

15. http://www.un.org/en/events/ruralwomenday/2011/sgmessage.shtml.02.09.2015.

16. http://www.unwomen.org/en/what-we-do/economic-empowerment/sustainable-development-and-climate-change#sthash.Vfzl9Myk.dpuf.03.09.2015.

17. www.un.org/popin/unfpa/taskforce/guide/iatfwemp.gdl.html.03.09.2015.

Chapter 2

Conceptualizing Motherhood in Ruby Langford's Don't Take Your Love to Town

ANNAPOORNA L.R.
Research Scholar
CES, JNU
New Delhi

Aboriginal motherhood is central to the larger socio-political stance of Australian women's life writings. Building upon the Aboriginal women's experiences and understanding of motherhood, Ruby Langford constructs a view of Aboriginal motherhood, in terms of both resistance and empowerment, totally different from the motherhood practiced and understood in the dominant Western culture. Consequently, Langford defines and positions motherhood in her life writing *Don't Take Your Love to Town* (1988) as a site of power for the Aboriginal women. Drawing upon Black feminist standpoint theories, in this paper I will attempt to detail how the tradition and practice of Aboriginal mothering portrayed in Ruby Langford's *Don't Take Your Love to Town* give rise to a distinct identity and political behaviour for the Australian Aboriginal women in the work.

Aboriginal women's standpoint inherently emerges from their everyday experiences which not only provides a clear–cut "angle of vision on self, community and society" but also effectuates the Aboriginal mother "to counter and interrupt the dominant discourse of black womanhood" (Tsosie 3). Patricia Hill Collins perspective on Black motherhood evidently provides a productive conceptual framework for examining Ruby Langford's portrayal of Aboriginal motherhood in her work. According to Collins, the "institution of Black motherhood consists of a series of constantly renegotiated and relationships" (Collins 176) that indigenous women experience with one another, with their children, with the larger indigenous community, and finally, with the self.

Ruby Langford depicts motherhood in her memoir in terms of an intense public and private endeavour. Interestingly, she defines mothering by largely emphasizing on the indigenous properties of Aboriginal womanhood. It is worth recalling Morrison's contention that "Black women… are providers and nurturers; they inhabit the public sphere of work and the private realm of home and do so unproblematically; they are both 'ship and safe harbor, inn and trail'" (O'Reilly 187). Langford in her memoir provides the reader a compelling view about the transmission of indigenous properties profoundly along the motherline and acquired by each generation of Aboriginal women. This primarily forms the crux of the Aboriginal women's empowerment. According to the critic Collins,

> …motherhood as an institution occupies a special place in transmitting values to children about their proper place. On the one hand, a mother can foster her children's oppression if she teaches them

to believe in their own inferiority. On
the other hand, the relationship between
mothers and children can serve as a private
sphere in which cultures of resistance and
everyday forms of resistance are learned…
When… [Aboriginal] mothers taught their
children to trust their own self-definitions
and value themselves, they offered a
powerful tool for resisting oppression (51).

The indigenous properties of womanhood also locate
Aboriginal mothers as "cultural bearers" (O'Reilly 188).
It can be observed that in this particular memoir, *Don't
Take Your Love to Town*, the Aboriginal mothers, including
Langford are deeply concerned with the preservation
of indigenous folklores and with sustaining productive
Aboriginal cultural beliefs and values. Her profound love
for her children can be indeed seen as an act of resistance.
This can be further substantiated by O' Reilly's view that
"Mother-love, in a racist culture that deems black children
unlovable, is thus an act of resistance" (O'Reilly 189). For
instance, when Langford and her step–mother Mum Joyce
attend their babies' boundless maternal love is celebrated.
She writes,

We sat these boys together and looked
at them. Beautiful black babies. Then Pearl
got up and took her first steps, waving
her arms like a bird flapping its wings
(Langford 70).

Such unbounded maternal love definitely conforms to O' Reilly's frame of reference as sites of resistance. Langford integrates mother–love and indigenous Aboriginal properties to effectuate both resistance and empowerment of Aboriginal women. Langford's portrayal of mother–love and Aboriginal mothering as resistance and empowerment trajectory can be examined under three main categories, namely, the practice of motherhood, the discourse of motherhood and the social identity of Aboriginal mother.

Regarding the practice of mothering much attention is needed on how "motherhood embraces both the 'apparently pre–social reality' of procreation and childbirth and 'its political historical institutionalisation' within specific– and diverse–social and cultural formations" (Walker 424). Mothering comprises diverse activities, namely, childbirth, physical and emotional care, involvement and protection, and also socialization. In her reflections on motherhood, Ruby Langford recounts her bush life, articulating a maternal identity that is totally different from the motherhood practiced and defined in the dominant culture. She writes,

> I'm alone in the bush with six kids. There are snakes and wild pigs around. I'm fifteen miles from the homestead and seventy miles from town. There's a car here, but I don't know the way to the homestead, there are tracks going off in all directions. If anything goes wrong, that's it… I told the kids to play close by and I kept watch for snakes. I killed four or five a day but they weren't poisonous ones (Langford 91).

Building upon her experiences Ruby Langford develops a notion of motherhood, which forms the essence of her larger political and philosophical view on Aboriginal womanhood.

Furthermore, an Aboriginal motherhood also embraces different shades of motherhood such as 'othermothering' and 'community mothering'. The term 'othermothering' primarily attributes to women caring a child who is not biologically related whereas 'community mothering' refers to women protecting and guarding the community. According to Collins, "othemothers ... traditionally have been central to the institution of Black motherhood" (178). The notion of 'othermothering' and 'community mothering' arise when Ruby Langford retrieves to her Aunt Nell's house in Bonalbo, who was the dominant maternal figure. The richness of the meaning attached to 'othermothering' gets also procured from the idea of Aboriginal mothers as healers. Ruby Langford in her memoir recounts the plight of unmothered and orphaned children whom she had taken under her care. Langford thus provides refreshing insights into the maternal warmth and sentiment when she performs the role of 'othermothering' to Terry Priest, Sparrow Freeman and Allan Barret. Referring to Allan, she says, "He grew up like a brother to my kids. I'm the only mother figure he's ever known" (Langford 164). The memoir explicitly demonstrates the influence of mothering on the emotional contentment of these children. Furthermore, Langford discloses how the psychological wound gets healed through the very act of mother-love and which essentially initiates them to self–love.

Aboriginal women appropriate the role of both the nurturer and preserver of the Aboriginal community. Black feminists believed that "Spirituality, history, and cultural recovery" are considered as the "provinces of the Black woman" (Stover 18). In fact, in the act of 'community mothering' the Aboriginal mother becomes the connective force in the community. As already mentioned one of the prime features that defines Aboriginal mothering is the socialization process. Socialization primarily refers to the transmission of Aboriginal traditional values and culture. Historically, the ethics of surviving the culture are mainly embedded in the dominance of Aboriginal mothers which is primarily by making a constant connection to the past generations through folklores and cultural practices. The spirit is what sustains the aborigines. It gives them hope and inspiration for the future. For instance, the critic Bill Edwards elucidates on Aboriginal understanding of spirituality. Accordingly he says, the "realm of spiritual existence is not divorced from the material world but is embedded in it" (82). There are several references in the memoir, which depicts occurrences where the spirits of the elders and relatives come as messengers and warn the loved ones. One such instance is when Langford claims that,

> I knew the house was full of spirits. When we were kids we used to hear the gate click shut, and footsteps on the veranda and down the hall. We weren't frightened, it was our home and they looked after us (Langford 63).

Similarly, at the time when she was distressed and tormented by the imminent possibility of losing her kids she felt the presence of her father's spirit consoling her. Subsequently, she writes,

> A wind was howling and blowing up the stairs, it was so strong it blew the bolt off the door. In my anguish I tossed and turned and was weeping as though my heart would break. Then I could sense my father's spirit, he was there, I could feel him patting my arm, comforting me. I fell into a deep sleep (Langford 103).

Furthermore, the concept of 'totem' that Langford explicates in her memoir is also an extension of the Aboriginal spirituality. The term 'totem' significantly points to the Aboriginal cultural belief of associating a specific Aboriginal clan with an animal or a plant that shares a common descent. Commenting on the significance of Aboriginal spirituality, Bill Edwards expounds on the intrinsic bond that the Aboriginal maintain with their immediate surroundings. Accordingly, he says, "… totemism point to important aspects of Aboriginal understandings about the presence of spiritual essence in the world and the relationship of people to other parts of the world" (Edwards 82).

Moreover, Ruby Langford's process of reasserting the traditional Aboriginal knowledge can be distinctly read along the lines of her larger critical project, decolonizing agenda. It is through the Aboriginal mothers that the passing on of the indigenous cultural values to each generation materializes. At this juncture, the critic

Judy Iseke's contention on spirituality as a mode of decolonization seems noteworthy. Iseke argues that,

> The dimension of spirituality in Indigenous knowledge provides the strength and power needed in physical communication. Indigenous knowledge forms are expressive and narrative. They are metaphorical in the use of proverbs, fables and tales. Indigenous knowledges view communalism as a mode of thought, emphasizing the sense of belongingness with a people and the land they share. It is not individualized and disconnected into universal abstract. It is grounded in a people and a place (36).

It is interesting to analyze how the Aboriginal women in the text are firmly tied to the "notions of land and community and cultural values of relationship and responsibility" (Tsosie 29). The point to emphasize is that, the belief in the spiritual entities such as spirits and 'totems' offers a much further dimension in the understanding of the Aboriginal community's identity. This also gets reflected in Partha Chatterjee's view that "the spiritual ... [is] an 'inner' domain bearing the 'essential' marks of cultural identity (6). For an Aboriginal woman's survival the "power of self-definition was essential" (Collins 1). They can attain self-definition primarily by embracing their powerful roles as mothers. It is they who are entrusted with the power to create in the minds of their kids the virtuous knowledge of Aboriginal culture. Moreover, they attain self-determination by the Aboriginal women's relationships with one another in providing a community feeling. Each of them inherently possesses the potential for cultural educators.

The discourse of motherhood evidently incorporates ideas such as womanhood, gender identity, and childhood. It is important to see how the discourse of Aboriginal motherhood attempts to challenge the dominant Western discourses of motherhood, specifically, the idea of 'good mother'. Within this focus, "the discourse of motherhood in many black, working-class communities may not emphasize women's involvement in the day-to-day care of their children as much as their responsibilities for financial support and discipline" (Walker 425). This specific contention on Black motherhood certainly echoes Langford's exposition of the Aboriginal motherhood. If there is an ineluctable force that governs her memoir, it is the strong bond between the Aboriginal women, namely motherhood and sisterhood. Langford presents Aboriginal womanhood as the central theme throughout the memoir. There are diverse instances in the memoir when Langford swears that she would not have survived without the community of Aboriginal women. The plight of Aboriginal mothers gets poignantly voiced through her. Langford in her work continuously problematizes motherhood rather than romanticizing it. Such an approach from her part constantly challenges the dominant discourse of motherhood. Contradictory to the dominant idea of 'good mother', Aboriginal women had to endure hardships which forced them to make anomalous compromises and thereby to resort to various actions. For instance, Langford in her anguish over losing her daughter, Pearl, began to drink excessively and it was her Koori friends, namely, Iris, Blue and Margaret who took care of her kids. Inevitably the motherhood and sisterhood in *Don't Take Your Love to Town* facilitate the Aboriginal women characters to carve their subjectivities, resist against victimization and fight for empowerment.

Finally, the social identity of the Aboriginal mother also firmly challenges the Eurocentric notion of Aboriginal women and concurrently assumes itself as a site for empowerment. According to the critic Cherryl Walker, social identity essentially "involves women's own construction of an identity as mothers— informed by the discourse of motherhood, mediated by the practice of mothering, but not simply a derivative of either" (426). Apparently, the Aboriginal women's construction of their social identity in Langford's *Don't Take Your Love to Town* overtly exposes Aboriginal women as agents of their indigenous cultural values and beliefs. The text mainly focuses on the "subjective dimension" of Aboriginal motherhood, primarily on how Aboriginal mothers perceive and experience themselves about the "role and relationship" (Walker 426) of motherhood. Furthermore, motherhood essentially provides a site for Aboriginal women where they can "express and learn the power of self–definition, the importance of valuing and respecting … the necessity of self-reliance and independence, and a belief in… [Aboriginal] women's empowerment" (Collins 176).

It goes without saying that, however personal it may appear Aboriginal motherhood in *Don't Take Your Love to Town* is inherently located in a social context where the Aboriginal mothers' identify themselves is viewed as a "part of a distinct social group" (Walker 426).

Langford immanently perceives Aboriginal motherhood as "providing a base for self-actualization" and more concretely "a catalyst for social activism" (Collins 176). As such, an Aboriginal mother's social role can also be located in her "degrees of creativity, reflection and choice" (Walker 427). Besides this understanding, Walker proposes that there is a concurrent play of social identities attached to an Aboriginal mother, namely, as a wife, worker, healer, Aboriginal, Black etc. Aboriginal women's "centrality is characterized less by the absence of husbands and fathers than by the significance of women. Though men may be physically present or have well–defined and culturally significant roles in the extended family, the kin units tends to be woman–centered" (Collins 178). Ruby Langford defines her relationship with her husband Gordon in very practical terms. She says,

> … though the association was wearing thin I tried to keep us together for the kids' sake. If he was using me I was using him just as much. My first priority was the kids and it helped to have someone bringing in a wage now and then (Langford 81).

In another instance she reflects on the predicament of Aboriginal women,

> … in the case of women living hard because it seemed like the men loved you for a while and then more kids came along and the men drank and gambled and disappeared. One day they'd had enough

and they just didn't come back. It happened with Gordon and later it happened with Peter, and my women friends all have similar stories (Langford 96).

Consequently, in such opposing circumstances, the alternate identities of an Aboriginal woman try to merge with the social identity of the mother resulting in the complex fashioning of women's choice. At this juncture, Giddens's assertion that 'reflexity' plays a crucial role in the construction of identity seems noteworthy. Accordingly, he argues that "Self-identity, in other words, is not something that is just given … but something that has to be routinely created and sustained in the reflexive activities of the individual" (Walker 427).

Ruby Langford in her memoir thus exposes how Aboriginal women develop an oppositional knowledge to the dominant ideologies by mainly participating as "mothers, othermothers, [community mothers], teachers" (Collins 10) in their Aboriginal community. Through their lived experiences that they specifically gained through their extended community and family, each Aboriginal woman constructs their own ideas about the concept of Aboriginal womanhood. Thus, Aboriginal women's self-definitions as mothers, othermothers, and community mothers, enabled them to reconstruct the notion of self and community. Such self-definitions of Aboriginal womanhood are often hailed by Black feminists as a political strategy to resist "the negative controlling images of Black womanhood advanced by Whites as well as the discriminatory social practices that these controlling images supported" (Collins 10).

WORKS CITED

Chatterjee, Partha. *The Nation and Its Fragments: Colonial and Postcolonial Histories.* New Jersey: Princeton UP, 1993. Print.

Collins, Patricia Hill. *Black Feminist Thought: Knowledge, Consciousness and Politics of Empowerment.* London: Routledge, 2000. Print.

Edwards, Bill. "Living the Dreaming". *Aboriginal Australia: An Introductory Reader in Aboriginal Studies.* Ed. Colin Bourke, Eleanor Bourke, Bill Edwards. Australia: University of Queensland Press, 2003. Print.

Giddens, A. *Modernity and Self-Identity.* London: Cambridge, 1991. Print.

Iseke, Judy. "Spirituality as Decolonizing". *Decolonization: Indigeneity, Education and Society.* 2.1 (2013): 35-54. Web 23 July 2014.

Langford, Ruby. *Don't Take Your Love to Town.* Australia: Penguin Books, 1989. Print.

O'Reilly, Andrea. *Toni Morrison and Motherhood: A Politics of the Heart.* Albany: State University of New York Press, 2004. Print.

Stover, Johnnie M. "Approaches to Morrison's Work: Feminist/Black Feminist". *The Toni Morrison Encyclopedia.* Ed. Elizabeth Ann Beaulieu. USA: Greenwood Press, 2003. Print.

Tsosie, Rebecca. "Native Women and Leadership: An Ethics of Culture and Relationship". Indigenous Women and Feminism: Politics, Activism, Culture. Ed. Cheryl Suzack, Shari M. Huhndorf, Jeanne Perreault, Jean Barman. Vancouver: UBC Press, 2010. Print.

Walker, Cherryl. "Conceptualising Motherhood in Twentieth Century South Africa". *Journal of Southern African Studies*. 21.3 (Sep 1995): 417-37. Web 9 July 2013.

Chapter 3

Expiation of Patriarchy through Matriarchal Resurgence: A Study of Oscillation of Power in John Steinbeck's *The Grapes of Wrath*

KEKA DAS
Assistant Professor & Head
Department of English
Vidyasagar College
39 Sankar Ghosh Lane
Kolkata - 700006

"What some people find in religion a writer may find in his craft…a kind of breaking through to glory."

- Steinbeck in a 1965 interview.

John Ernst Steinbeck indeed traversed glorious avenues as "The Grapes of Wrath" (Winner of the Pulitzer Prize in 1940) turned out to be the finest of his seventeen novels. Set in the backdrop of Dust Bowl Oklahoma and Californian migrant life, Steinbeck's "The Grapes of Wrath" traces the poignant journey of the Joads who, displaced, dispossessed and uprooted, travel west in search of The Promised Land. Being a votary of Socialism and an avid critic of Capitalistic economy, Steinbeck shared utmost sympathy with the uprooted migrants and their insurmountable predicaments, as evinced by the Joads and their struggle with inexorable circumstances that threaten to tear asunder all their hopes yet they hang on like the legendary last leaf, under the munificence of human spirit that simply refuses to give up. In a series of Articles authored by Steinbeck for the "San Francisco Chronicle", Steinbeck shares his personal observation of migrant camps that he had obtained in course of his extensive travels:

> "The migrants are needed, and they are hated. Arriving in a district they find the dislike always meted out by the resident to the foreigner, the outlander... The migrants are hated for the following reasons, that they are ignorant and dirty people, that they are carriers of disease, that they increase the necessity for police and the tax bill for schooling in a community, and that if they are allowed to organize they can, simply by refusing to work, wipe out a season's crop." (Steinbeck, Harvest Gypsies 20)

Steinbeck was wary of the seeming lackadaisical attitude of people towards suffering humanity; he therefore desperately wanted to rouse them from their state of slumber; "I am not writing a satisfying story," Steinbeck says to Pascal Covici on January 16, 1939:"I've done my damndest to rip a reader's nerves to rags; I don't want him satisfied... I tried to write this book the way lives are being lived not the way books are written…Throughout I've tried to make the reader participate in the actuality, what he takes from it will be scaled entirely on his own depth or hollowness. There are five layers in this book, a reader will find as many as he can and he won't find more than he has in himself."

Steinbeck has thus woven a timeless human drama on tapestries of 'false hopes, thwarted desires and broken dreams'; his undisputed masterpiece indeed scales the pinnacle of pathos as 'an eloquent tribute to the endurance and dignity of the human spirit.'

Steinbeck situates the novel in the backdrop of Dust-bowl Oklahoma (This novel being the third and final part of Steinbeck's famed Dust-bowl Trilogy.), a 'Wasteland' of hopelessness and all-subsuming gloom where Nature, the macrocosm, is visualized as a 'pestilence-striken' "red country"; in "part of the gray country" of Oklahoma, "last rains gently cut the scarred earth…plough crossed, re-crossed the rivulet marks"; Steinbeck here dexterously intersperses macrocosm with microcosm (nature and man) to impregnate nature with the pulsating warmth of human life. William Wordsworth, high-priest of Romanticism, had visualized life in swirling rings of smoke over a thick canopy of beechen foliage; Steinbeck too celebrates the invincibility of human spirit amidst widespread gloom and nihilism of modern 'Wasteland'. Description of nature gradually leads to a climax, setting the tone of the novel. "… roots were freed by the prying wind";"The dawn came, but no day"; "In the gray sky a red sun appeared,…" ;"The wind cried and whimpered over the fallen corn". Interestingly, Steinbeck constantly visualizes nature as a woman and ragged, suffering Mother Earth is an externalization of subjugated womanhood. "And the women came out of the house to stand beside their men-to feel whether this time the men would break. The women studied the men's faces secretly, for the corn could go, as long as something else remained…"- etch out in glaring terms a bitter reality; women existed as merely the 'Other' of their male folks, hardly ever being allowed any say in important matters concerning household or decision-making. "Like *In Dubious Battle* and *Of Mice and Men, The Grapes of Wrath* is a novel fully immersed in the patriarchal tradition of portraying the world seen through the eyes of men, emphasizing the relationships of men to each other and to the rest of the world (McKay 50)." (Burri119). "After a while the faces of the watching men lost their bemused perplexity and became hard and angry and resistant. Then the women knew that there was no break. Then they asked, "What'll we do?" And the man replied, "I don't know". But it was all right, and the watching children knew it was all right. Women and children knew deep in themselves that no misfortune was too great to bear if their men were whole." or "Open doors…women stood looking out-watched their men talking to the owner men. They were silent." or "In the doorways of the sun beaten tenant houses, women sighed and then shifted feet so that the one that had been down was now on top, and the toes working." or even "The women moved cautiously out of the doorways toward their men, …ready to run. After a time the women asked,…"- all such statements are poignant pointers of silent, subservient, passive role of women who always watched perplexed and figuring men, waiting for them to arrive at a decision or take action. However, Steinbeck dexterously builds up the monument of hierarchical hegemony envisaged by an essentially patriarchal society that assigned subservient roles to women, only to systematically dissipate it in course of the novel, thereby refuting claims of several critics that Steinbeck was a misogynist.

In 1974, the French writer Francoise d' Eaubonne drew a semblance between nature and women and applied the term 'Eco-Feminism' to the philosophy that women have a spiritual connection with nature that is stronger than men, that women and nature are dominated by men in similar ways, and that women's connections to nature can be a source of strength. Steinbeck is particularly fond of men who earn their bread with sweat of their brow, working ceaselessly in open fields amidst mountains. They have always appealed to him as individuals, as an object that addresses his "esthetic sense" so much for the men in his works. As far as women are concerned, he likes to see and project them nursing their babies. However, an eco-feministic study of his works does reveal that Steinbeck's women share an almost umbilical connection with nature, at times women and nature are exploited and controlled by Steinbeck's men in similar ways and, women fall back on nature and draw sustenance, emotional and spiritual succour whenever they need to resuscitate their sagging spirit. Steinbeck mentions that for soil testing, cumbersome machines are employed; such a tampering with Mother Earth is almost tantamount to a symbolic rape, a gross violation of her sanctity. Evidently, Nature would wrench her due from man and dust-storms were almost pre-ordained. Imagery of sexual violation continues in the line- "The land bore under iron and under iron it died"; both Mother Earth and women unobtrusively and silently suffer the bulldozing of patriarchal authorities that are insensitive to the needs and desires of women and Nature, often exploiting them for garnering personal benefits. Yet, their helplessness in the face of inexorable machines driven by steel-hands of authorities is amply evident: "The tenant man stared after it, his rifle in his hand. His wife was beside him, and the quiet children behind. And all of them stared after the tractor." As a woman, the wife was doubly marginalized, reeling under a subservient role meted out to her by the patriarchal society. For this reason perhaps, the dilapidated house has been likened to a woman in Chapter-6: "Let's look in the house, she's all pushed out a shape. Something knocked the hell out of her." The image of destroyed house sans any inhabitants again refers to sterile women who are incapable of bearing children. Steinbeck accords fastidiously compartmentalized role to women-either that of a mother, daughter, wife, or a whore existing on the precipice of human society. A sterile woman is therefore redundant in Steinbeck's world.

Strangely enough, men have been depicted as timid, weak, figuring and confused; some of the men portrayed by Steinbeck are not too happy with obvious sexist stratifications imposed by our society. As Uncle John thinks aloud, had he not been fifty and one of the natural rulers of the family, he would have liked Rose to take up the honour seat beside the driver as she was pregnant. Sad and alienated on having lost his wife early, he often lusted for, snorted and rutted on unresponsive bodies of whores. Uncle John holds himself responsible for the death of his fine, good wife as he had refused to fetch a doctor for her when she complained of stomach ache as he thought it was caused by over-eating. Interestingly, as the novel progresses, we find its men either dying or abandoning the family; it was then left to Joad women to carry the mantle of Joads'; "When examining The Grapes of Wrath, however, it becomes clear that women play a central role and are needed in a time of crisis. Warren Motley argues that in this novel, Steinbeck, influenced by anthropologist Robert Briffault's theories on the matriarchal origin of society, reverses the patriarchal tradition as he portrays the Joad family as shifting from a patriarchal structure to a predominantly matriarchal one (397)." (Burri 120)

From Tom Joad and Casy, the preacher's conversation, their intense carnal desires emerge as they derive deep sadistic pleasure by discussing about female body-parts; Casy even scribbles female body-parts on sand without any face; evidently, they were least concerned about the face as they were solely inclined towards gratification of senses-"I'd take one of them girls out in the grass, an I'd lay with her…" Although Casy's urge for sexual gratification as an individual is perfectly understandable, his desires as a preacher bring to focus hypocrisy of preachers and meaninglessness of dogmatic religion-"There ain't nothing like a good hot meetin' for pushing' 'em over.", he said, "I done that myself." or "pullin' little girls' pigtails…", "You was all wropped up in yankin' that pigtail out by the roots" To this Casy retorts "You wasn't a preacher. A girl was just a girl to you…But to me they was holy vessels. I was savin' their souls." However, Tom's justification for his smouldering lust can't be overlooked- "I been a long time without a girl," he said. "It's gonna take some catchin' up." "That preacher's missus took a godawful poundin' after ever' night meetin'" Casy's response is pregnant with a deep philosophical overtone; "There ain't no sin and there ain't no virtue." ;You give her a goin' –over," he said.

"You figured her out."; "pullin' pigtail…Susy Little…She bust my finger a year later." Tom Joad makes a blatant confession "…I was goddamn glad when I got one" as it "Makes it hard not havin' no women." Tom Joad keeps the turtle that he had picked up en route, tightly under wraps as it tries to budge; the desperate writhing of the turtle to get free can be read as a commentary on the condition of women, as Casy rightfully says, 'What you got there-a chicken? You 'll smother it.' Tom clarifies that that was an old turtle he had taken for the kids as kids like turtles.

One of the phenomenal women characters in the oeuvre of Steinbeck, towering as the epitome of courage, perseverance, practicalism, self-less love and sacrifice, Ma Joad is introduced from Tom's viewpoint. She is shown as a homemaker in complete control of the family. 'The first time she is introduced, she is "engaged with the most symbolic act of mothering- feeding her family" (McKay 60). The second time, she is seen washing clothes, and the third time she is trying to dress the difficult and unreasonable Grampa Joad. These activities represent the most important tasks of a woman: feeding the family, keeping them clean, and taking care of their needs (60).' (Burri124). The house Joads left behind still had traces of things used by women or reminded of women. The bedroom had picture of an Indian girl and a woman's high-button shoe that is reminiscent of Ma for Tom. Its curled up at toe and broken over instep, symbolizing over-use and hard physical labour she is subjected to. He says Ma liked her shoes. As the family has moved on, they have carried the bare essentials; Ma had to forego hers to lighten the family's burden. Or she could be a practical headed woman who lets go of encumbrances and acts well and wisely in trying circumstances, as she does by concealing the dead body of Granma to facilitate smoothing crossing-over of the Joads' truck. Ma seems to be a no-nonsense go-getter strong woman who only means business without slightest touch of any feminine softness. Once she had beaten the hell out of a tin peddler who had dared to argue with her, even going to the extent of attempting to cut his head off. Ma had said that the preacher Casy could be trusted. Ma's premonition that she will never see Tom, again, proves to be true by the end of the novel as Tom leaves the family, to escape from law into an uncertain, unknown world of freedom. Tom remembers his mother's voice as "cool, calm drawl, friendly and humble". (pp.77)

Although not fat, Ma was heavy with child-bearing and work. Although Steinbeck is often accused of being a misogynist who liked the women to be child-bearers and nurturers of families, in one small description he situates Ma to where she actually belongs-the controller of the family and she herself knows it too well. She knew that the Joad family, for not to fail, she had to somehow hang on. So much dependent was the family on her that she was the one who decided if she was joyous. Above all, years of grinding pain and sufferings had matured her to the level of resignation, like Maurya. She was cool, calm and composed. She is referred to as an ''arbiter' and a 'goddess' but not as a Leader. (pp. 79) From her initial reactions on seeing Tom who had been released on parole, we do realize that her essential motherly softness is still at work. It is not altogether defunct now. Yet, within seconds she gathers herself and wonders about Tom's freedom. Her essential womanly soft feelings have been suppressed by the pressure of trying times. The eagerness, the sense of anticipation, her ceaseless questions, amply bring out her latent motherly feelings and anxiety for Tom which hitherto was incomprehensible. (pp 80) Ma's tenacity and perseverance and never-say-die attitude was more than evident when she consoles her son- "Tommy, don't you go fightin' 'em alone. They'll hunt you down like a coyote. Tommy, I got to thinkin' an' dreamin' an' wonderin'." Even her son seems to be amazed at her new-found sense of strength- "you never was like this before!" To this, her answer was precise- "I never had my house pushed over," or "I never had my fambly stuck out on the road. I never had to sell-ever'thing-". In a moment, she becomes business-like-preparing food for the family. Steinbeck presents her as a source of sustenance, not only physical but also emotional. She happens to be the emotional mainstay of the family. "It is furthermore significant that the tools of the men's labour, such as the horses and ploughs are sold before the journey, but Ma Joad's tools, the household goods, are brought along, and become of vital importance to the family's survival. Thus, she takes on the masculine role of the provider, while the men continue to sit around uselessly, unable to perform their traditional duties. While Ma Joad's power increases the further they travel from their home, the opposite is true for Pa Joad, the family patriarch and the other men in the family. Motley argues since power is linked to the ability to work, and as the men have lost this ability with the emergence of the crisis, the power and authority has been transferred to the women." (Burri123) The fact that she repeatedly compares the prisoner, who was killed at a fabricated pretext, again highlights man's domination and ceaseless killing of animals.

Steinbeck introduces the character of Granma who survives only because her husband does; when her husband, our Grampa dies, she follows suit. The idea being she is incapable of sustaining herself independently, shorn of her identity as an individual, merely existing as a shadow. Strangely, it was fighting that kept their relationship going. Slightly weird as she was, her husband better avoided her and did not try to torture her as children do to bugs, when she fired a shotgun at him. However, the readers are shocked at a shocking revelation – she had received tortures from her equally 'mean' husband.

Steinbeck strikes a note of intense pathos in Chapter 9 where women seem to be deliberating burning or not burning their prized possessions 'To be or not to be/ That is the question'. Being allowed to, or rather able to, circumscribed by circumstances, carry only the bare essentials, the women are left to make the most difficult and heart-wrenching choices of their lives- they go for 'a few pots to cook and wash in', mattresses, lantern, buckets and a piece of canvas for making a tent, kerosene can, even a rifle, as they make a chilling confession-"When shoes and clothes and food, when even hope is gone, we'll have the rifle". They shove off their emotions in lieu of materialistic considerations for family- their mementos reminding them of their fathers, aunts and others, and burn them. "How can we live without our lives? How will we know it's us without our past? No. Leave it. Burn it." Before leaving for California, she set on fire the box containing her most prized possessions as she had realized their inability to accommodate more stuff onto the truck. However, she doesn't let go all her stuff, tucking into her dress pocket some trinkets that she could afford to carry without anyone noticing it.

Ma, one of most memorable women creations of Steinbeck, is portrayed as rigid and freckled from the routine household chores that she performs unquestioningly for the family. Yet it is only she who had the foresight to question the high promises beckoning from their Promised Land. She might be confined within four walls of her household, yet she was extremely intelligent, practical, thoroughly a family-centric woman who had taken the reins of the Joad family without the Joad patriarchs even realizing it. Yet she is not shorn of high dreams about their migration to California where they could have small white houses amidst orange orchards where they would yell their guts out while picking oranges. Yet she was fully aware of the rightful 'right' of men when she looked to Tom to speak when Casy expressed his desire to go along with the Joads to the West, because he was a man but Tom did not speak. She let him have the chance that was his right, and then she said, "Why, we'd be proud to have you. 'Course I can't say right now; Pa says all the men'll talk tonight and figger when we gonna start. I guess maybe we better not say till all the men come." She tactfully handles the situation by leaving the ultimate decision to be made on Men folks, yet subtly gives her opinion in the affirmative by saying that he would be only too welcome if there is room enough in the truck. When the family had to make important decisions, the men squatted, women-folks standing behind them. Rather than being a family norm, this was a social construct. Even weaker and unconfident men like Al stood behind women for strength; Grampa being the titular head was required to comment first, how silly it would be nevertheless. When the family was in a fix about Casy, Ma again clarifies the matter diplomatically by stating that Joads can't be that mean enough to not take him and one more can certainly be squeezed in as twelve will be going although there is room for only six. Although not the head, Ma is considered most powerful in the group. When Casy volunteers to help her in kitchen work, she says firmly-"It's women's work." To this, Casy's reply is significant; "It's all work…They's too much of it to split it up to men's or women's work." Rather being suppressed and dominated by man, it is their pre-conceived notions as subsidiary to men that have kept them firmly entrenched in their subservient, well-etched out womanly roles as prescribed by society. Although Tom dismisses her demeanor as mere tiredness, Casy sees through her tiredness. What follows, climbs the height of pathos and self- sacrifice that only women are capable of. She again shows super-human resilience when she rests with the dead body of Granma, even going to the extent of concealing her death from authorities and other family members to facilitate smooth passage towards their Promised Land. When her family gets to know that, she had laid quietly all night with Granma's dead body only to ensure smooth passage for the family, "The family looked at Ma with a little terror at her strength." Grampa and Granma were seemingly distraught at having been displaced and dispossessed at the wee hours of their lives, Ma had never betrayed signs of any emotion. Yet this feeling had also subsumed her as she tried to look back to the place they were perhaps leaving forever for good and her eyes were soon overwhelmed with a sense of weariness.

In course of her journey to the Promised Land, Al asks Ma if she is scared of going and she answers in a tone of finality, "When somepin happens that I got to do somepin-I'll do it." She is only too aware of her family's dependence on her only for pork bones; she knows that they would get upset if "I done any more'n that." She also acts as a pillar of strength for ailing Granma. Ma's humane side is revealed when she serves stew to wolvish starving children at the camp, yet she is diligent enough to not let her family go hungry, especially Rosasharn as she was going to have a baby. She is sensible enough to not let Pa talk ill of Connie in Rose's presence as that might have ill-effect on the unborn child. When the Joads embark on their westward journey, men lose their work and eventually, they are saddled with hopelessness and despair; women, on the other hand, do carry on their work of immanence, providing the family with succour in moments of extreme crisis (McKay 55). "As activity is traditionally associated with the masculine, and passivity with femininity, the traditional gender roles are reversed, as the men are reduced into passivity while the women remain active. Thus, the shift from patriarchy to matriarchy seems appropriate in this situation./ Indeed, Ma Joad, the family matriarch, proves to be a pillar of strength and a cohesive force in the family, and she readily takes on the role of authority when the men around her fail to assert theirs." (Burri122)

Rose of Sharon, her daughter, too takes up the role of a saviour in the ultimate Chapter when she suckles a dying man; her baby might have perished but she lives on, reminiscent of Mother Mary; "Rambold notes that Rose of Sharon's nursing of the starving man is filled with biblical allusions to the coming of the new heaven and new earth described in the book of the prophet Isaiah:

> *Rejoice ye with Jerusalem, and be glad*
> *with her, all ye that love her, rejoice for joy*
> *with her, all ye that mourn for her: That ye*
> *may suck, and be satisfied with the breasts of*
> *her consolations; that ye may milk out, and*
> *be delighted with the abundance of her glory.*
> *For thus saith the Lord, Behold, I will extend*
> *peace to her like a river, and the glory of the*
> *Gentiles like a flowing stream; and then shall*
> *ye suck, ye shall be borne upon her sides, and*
> *be dandled upon her knees. As one whom*
> *his mother comforteth, so I will comfort you;*
> *and ye shall be comforted in Jerusalem. (Isa.*
> *66:10-13)" (Burri129).*

Even her name resonates with Biblical allusions. "The first part of her name, Rose, is a traditional symbol of perfection, and alludes to the image of the cup of eternal life. As a Christian symbol, the rose, with its thorns, symbolizes the suffering of Christ and his love for humanity (Tresidder 162). In the Bible, Sharon is a place of beauty, emblematic of fertility, and the name itself means floral or fertile plains (Jones 325). Furthermore, the phrase or name Rose of Sharon is taken directly from Song of Songs (2:1), where it can be interpreted as the perfect flower and a symbol of God (Kennedy 22)." "…by offering the sacramental gift of herself she embodies the symbol of resurrection and thus becomes a Christ-like figure (Crockett 198-199)." (Burri 128). The dying man is emblematic of suffering humanity waiting for deliverance at the hands of a woman. 'Martin Shockley says that this scene essentially depicts Rose of Sharon's rite of passage, as well as her surrender, as she in effect says "Not my will, but Thine be done" (89). Shockley further likens this scene to the Holy Communion, as Rose of Sharon

> *gives what Christ gave… The ultimate mystery of the Christian religion is realized through [her]… She smiles mysteriously because what has been mystery is now knowledge. This is my body, says [Rose of Sharon], and becomes the Resurrection and the Life. Rose of Sharon, the life-giver… In her, death and life are one, and through her, life triumphs over death. (89)*

Thus, according to the biblical interpretations of her character, Rose of Sharon becomes the archetypal Madonna, the patriarchal idealization of the feminine.' (Burri 130) In this context, says Adair, 'Rose of Sharon's body becomes "pure spectacle; a safe act of lack and mutilation to be looked at without fear, at once both telos and origin of man's desire" (51). This scene, Adair argues, is of great significance in "a patriarchy in disarray", as the female, a mother and a wife, is able to position herself as a sexualized, yet safe spectacle (51)' (Burri 131).

Rose of Sharon has also been carefully portrayed by Steinbeck; "Shy, quiet, uncertain and dependent, Rose of Sharon embodies the traditional notions of the feminine, and consequently possesses no power within the family. The fact that her pregnancy enables her to receive preferential treatment at times reinforces the idea of the sacredness of motherhood, which exists in patriarchal culture, which further serves to enslave her, according to de Beauvoir (560)"

(Burri 123). She is now extra careful because of the baby she carries in her womb-her braided hair made an ash-blond crown around her soft, round, erstwhile voluptuous and inviting face. But now her face seems to have put a barrier of pregnancy. In fact her whole body had become demure and serious, much to the dismay of Connie, her husband. For her, "the world was pregnant…" and "she thought only in terms of reproduction and of motherhood."'This kind of behaviour, according to de Beauvoir, is also typical of a pregnant woman, who now "experiences the satisfaction of feeling 'interesting', which has been, since her adolescence, her deepest desire;… at present, she is no longer sex object or servant, but she embodies the species, she is the promise of life, of eternity;…Justified by the presence within her of another, she finally fully enjoys being herself (558)' (Burri 127) Whereas Connie was frightened and bewildered for no longer receiving sexual favours from her, Rose is much more concerned about the baby than him. Connie even leaves her in course of their journey; when she finally loses her child, she has no one to provide succor. He fails to be with her at the moment of utmost crisis in her life, although she had been extremely proud of him, as evident from her 'grand' way of introducing him to Tom. One of the reasons why she lost her baby could be that they had got intimate while travelling on truck, in advanced stage of her pregnancy. Evidently Connie had become one of the dissenting forces in the family that needed to be expelled. When their dog was writhing with excruciating pain on being hit by a speeding car, Rose begged to know if that will hurt. Even Ruthie was shocked. However, it was Winfield who threw up. Evidently, women, although more sensitive, knew how to keep their swirling emotions in check. Again, quite contrary to expectations, Ma is asked by Pa to lay out Grampa's mortal remains and Sairy volunteers to get supper for him. In an almost superhuman show of strength, she cleans him, dresses him and decides to wrap him in an old quilt taken from Sairy. However the readers get a hint of Ma's inner self disintegrating when she sways a little after getting Grampa's body ready for a decent burial. When Rose expressed their desire to not live in the country, Ma was shocked at their decision to not live with the family. Being impractical, Rose is not tenacious enough to understand that her thoughts were all a dream. Being extremely practical and family-centric, Ma insists on staying with the family as a unit. She warns-"It ain't good for folks to break up." Yet, "As the family's economic and moral reserves dwindle, the family unit itself breaks up:

> Grampa Joad dies before they are out of Oklahoma and lies in a nameless grave; Granma is buried a pauper; Noah deserts the family; Connie deserts Rosasharn; the baby is born dead; Tom becomes a fugitive; Al is planning to leave as soon as possible; Casey is killed; and they are forced to abandon the Wilsons.(Lisca, *The Grapes of Wrath as Fiction* 306)" (Burri 118)

When Ma finds Granma in a deplorable condition, she puts her foot down and holds back the family from moving further. Wielding the jack-handle, she brandishes it and takes control of the whole situation- Immediately the group knew that "Ma had won. And Ma knew it too." she was the power-impersonate and she had taken control of the family now; expiation of patriarchy through resurgence of matriarchy has now been fully achieved.

An immaculate understanding of Steinbeck's text corroborates that rather than patriarchy, it is sexist stratification that keeps women obdurately entrenched in stereotypical gender-based roles prescribed by the society. Steinbeck too conforms to this patriarchal ideology within the literary cannon. However, his Pulitzer Prize -winning text, peopled by women who are amalgamation of opposite traits, is phenomenal as it portrays a gradual and inevitable shift of power-crux to matriarchy. Keeping in mind the Hindu philosophy of 'ardhya-nariswar', it is only a peaceful co-existence with mutual understanding and respect between man and woman that our civilization can surge ahead, riding high on the wings of unflinching hope and undying optimism.

WORKS CITED

1. Primary Source
   i) Steinbeck, John. The Grapes of Wrath. Penguin Books, 2000. Print.

2. Secondary Sources
   i) Burri, Stella. The Silenced Women of John Steinbeck's Dustbowl Trilogy. Dissertation supervisor Dr. Dianne Shober, 2012.
   ii) Butler, Judith. "Sex and Gender in Simone de Beauvoir's *Second Sex*". Yale French Studies: Simone de Beauvoir: Witness to a Century. 72 (1986): 35-49. Print.
   iii) Crocket, *H. Kelly. "The Bilbe and The Grapes of Wrath." College English. 24.3 (1962): 193-199. Print.*
   iv) *De Beauvoir, Simone. The Second Sex. 1948. London: Vintage Press, 2010. Print.*
   v) *Gilbert, Sandra M. & Susan Gubar. The Madwoman in the Attic- The Woman Writer and the Nineteenth-Century Literary Imagination. 2nd Ed. New Haven: Yale University Press, 2000. Print.L*
   vi) *Lisca, Peter. "The Grapes of Wrath as Fiction." PMLA. 72.1 (1957): 296-309. Print.*
   vii) *McKay, Nellie Y. "Happy [?]-Wife-and-Motherdom: The Portrayal of Ma Joad in John Steinbeck's The Grapes of Wrath." Bloom's Modern Critical Views:*

John Steinbeck. Harold Bloom. Ed. New York: Infobase Publishers, 2008. 47-70. Print.

viii) *Motley, Warren. "From Patriarchy to Matriarchy: Ma Joad's Role in The Grapes of Wrath." American Literature. 54.3 (1982): 397-412. Print.*

ix) *Rombold, Tamara "Biblical Inversion in The Grapes of Wrath." College Literature. 14.2 (1987): 146-166. Print.*

x) *Shockley, Martin. "Christian Symbolism in The Grapes of Wrath." College English. 18.2 (1956): 87-90. Print.*

xi) *Jones, Alfred. Dictionary of Old Testament Proper Names. Grand Rapids: Kregel. 1997. Print.*

xii) *Kennedy, Katherine. Christian Symbols. New York: Kressinger, 2003. Print.*

xiii) *Tressider, Jack. The Watkins Dictionary of Symbols. London: Watkins, 2008. Print.*

xiv) *Adair, Vivyan C. From Good Ma to Welfare Queen:* A Genealogy of the Poor Woman in America. New York: Garland Publishing, 2000. Print.

Chapter 4

The Spatial Politics of Home in Shashi Deshpande's *That Long Silence*

JAYANTA RANA
Assistant Prof. in English,
Netaji Satabarshiki Mahavidyalaya,
Ashoknagar, Habra,
24 Parganas (North) West Bengal, India.

Home is primarily conceived of as a geographical space but significantly it is also vital as "an ideal and an imaginary that is imbued with feelings." [1] Somerville (1992) has picked out seven key aspects of being at home: shelter, hearth, (emotional and physical well-being), heart (loving and caring relations), privacy, roots (source of identity and meaning, fullness), abode and paradise (ideal home as distinct from everyday life).[2] Far away from the surveillance and hostility of the outside world, home is imagined as a safe haven for individuals. It is within the four walls and through the various objects of a home, an individual has given expression to his or her emotions ideas and beliefs.

Shashi Deshpande(b.1938) has been writing steadily since early 1970s and through her stories and novels, she has consistently focused on middle class female characters in domestic settings. The writings are honest case studies of how this section of women fares in a dominant patriarchal society and how their choices in life are crucially mediated by the spatial economy and politics of the both parental and marital homes. In her works, home, is thus imagined within stories of belonging, desire, affection and intimacy but there are also feelings of fear, violence and corroding sense of emotional alienation. Her fifth novel, *That Long Silence* (1988) again puts the female protagonist in the middle of a personal crisis that forces her to withdraw from her routine domesticated existence, leading to a new realization of herself and an attendant recognition of her relationships.

That Long silence is the story of a housewife, Jaya, who is forced to negotiate the power- hierarchy for the first time in her life. Written in the first person confessional mode, the emphasis is on how the protagonist responds to the spatial politics at home which defines a woman through a series of gendered roles and responsibilities. Through the course of the novel, Deshpande is able to show how Jaya, at first, realizes marriage is an autonomous power game and then decides to claim privacy for herself within the gendered space of home itself.

This paper focuses on the struggle of Jaya who ultimately helps herself to a new realization and reorganisation of her rules and priorities if not a material change at the end. In the process, the protagonist comes to question a few issues on her own as home, the geographical idea, takes on the identity of "a hybrid place composed of emotional spatial and psychological fragments."[3]

If home is crucial to an individual's idea of self, then, it is still very much a man's world. Marion Young (1997) brings in Luce Irigaray's ideas to explore the gendering of home:

> "…man can build and dwell in the world in patriarchal culture [Irigaray suggests] only on the basis of materiality and nurturance of women. In the idea of 'Home', man projects onto woman, the nostalgic longing for the lost wholeness of the original mother. To fix and keep hold of his identity man makes a house, puts things in it and confines there his woman who reflects his identity to him. The price she pays for supporting this subjectivity, however, is dereliction, having no self of her own".[4]

Irigaray, here, emphasizes how home gets gendered as a woman complies with the male ideas and priorities of home. Young, on the other hand, puts four important aspects of home that should be ideally available to people if they belong to that home: "safety, individuation whereby each individual has place for the basic activities of life, privacy; and preservation."[5].

However, these attributes of an ideal home is more often denied to a woman –inside a home a woman is not safe, not an individual and her privacy is not secured. This gendered nature of home is under close scrutiny in Deshpande's *That Long Silence*.

The novel begins with the crisis in Jaya's life as her husband, Mohan, gets entangled in a high level corruption. That means the couple has to lie low for the time being.

As they decide to relocate themselves in an empty flat in
another part of the city, they have enough time to confront
themselves. In the absence of children, while Mohan tries
to validate himself as the dedicated family head, his wife
decides to go back and forth into the past and the present
to know how she has travelled in her various capacities as
a daughter, a wife and a mother. In all her role-playing,
however, the spatial constraint plays `a crucial part. In
other words, how she finds herself now has always been
decided upon by the degree of spatial independence she
had within that home space.

In a patriarchal set up, if marital home is dominantly
associated with hostility and indifference, then, parental
home, in a binary code, promises not only shelter but also a
kind of understanding of a woman's predicament. Chandra
(2008) emphasizes these aspects of a parental house in
these lines:

> "As a site of nostalgia, a home allows
> a return to an eternal childhood-security
> and as well as defined limits."[6]

Jaya's memories of childhood are no different. Her
parental home had her secured but all along it had been a
training ground for her- a life with 'defined limits'. Radio
Ceylon and its broadcast of popular Hindi songs were, thus,
deemed as 'poor taste'. Instead of this 'disgusting mush' of
pop songs, she was encouraged to appreciate Indian classical
music. Her father did try earnestly to make her love the
classical masters like Faiyaz Khan instead of Rafi and Lata,
the legendary king and queen of Hindi film music. This,
however, did not deter her from enjoying what she loved.

Then, in her marital life, she dared not express her fascination for popular advertisements for fear of being getting dismissed as a woman with 'cheap' popular tastes. However, in both cases, she continued to enjoy furtively what she liked in life:

> "I did [like the advertisements] but I never dared to confess it to him [her husband]. What if he too said, "what poor taste you have, Jaya…".[7]

If a parental home provides shelter, supper and security to a girl child, it also decides in the most crucial decision of her life- her marriage. This is through marriage a woman has to leave the temporary parental shelter –a *sarai*-for her permanent marital home:

> "…as we grew into young women, we realized it was not love, but marriage that was the destiny waiting for us."[8]

If as a young woman, she nurtured romantic dreams her parents turned those 'vague desires' into 'hard facts' of an arranged marriage.

Marital home is, unequivocally, a gendered space whereby people are differently positioned in relation to their gender resulting in different forms of lived reality. Massey (1991) has used the term 'power geometry' to underline this gendering of marital homes:

> "…places are shaped by power geometry, whereby different individuals

are placed in very distinct ways in relation
to these flows and interconnections."[9]

Jaya, in Deshpande's novel, thus, experiences the marital home in isolation, listens to what her husband Mohan has to say and tries to create a different identity in relation to the objects around her within the four walls of her confined space. Her husband, Mohan, is supposed to be her 'sheltering tree' and, thus, she does what she can to 'be good to Mohan'. He expects total submission in line with the rules of a marital home. Thus, Jaya's roles as a wife and a mother soon take up all her time. Consequently, her life gets reduced into a long wait for the people:

"Wait until your husband comes, wait
until you have kids. Yes ever since I got
married I had done nothing but wait."[10]

In fact, the children become the 'sacred cow' in a married woman's life: "the justification for everything even for living." These entire role playing mean less choice and lesser spatial and mental freedom to work out what a woman ultimately looks for in life. However, if a marriage is taken as 'two bullocks yoked together', then, like a sane animal, a woman decides finally not to go her own ways: 'what animal would voluntarily choose pain.'[11]

And when a woman behaves differently from the set norms, death is a distinct possibility. Kusum, thus, throws her into a wall as she was 'of no use to anyone'.

A home is also a place where a woman's spirit is domesticated and her life gets lost in the endless chores of the household. In the institution of marriage, these household jobs are vital but they are at the same time condemned as paltry in comparison to a man's job in the outside world. Dolores Hayden (2002), in these lines, tries to understand what domestic work involves:

> "Each household has a kitchen and laundry to clean, and separate living areas require the individual supervision of children. They also involve nurturing activities: cooking, home remedies for illnesses, emotional support for family members, arranging recreational activities, keeping in touch with relatives, interaction with business(shops) and institutions(schools).But all these are unrecognized".[12]

The 'power geometry' at work, in a patriarchal home, ensures that the lion-share of domestic work is taken care of by women while men have enough leisure to indulge their passions. Mohan, thus, can refuse to cook at home but glorifies his work outside home. His privilege as the bread-earner of the family means he is entitled to his rest after a hard day's work but his wife is bound to take care of children all through the day. This clear demarcation between a woman working inside and man working outside the home space has received critical attention from Partha Chatterjee too:

> "The home in its essence must remain unaffected by the profane activities of

the material world –and woman is its
representation."[13]

This is why, as Chatterjee says, men and women
act as per their gender roles, leading to a clear division
between the home and the world. Therefore, the
domestic responsibilities continue to remain a woman's
duty. Deshpande's protagonist is one such woman who
scrubs and cleans and 'takes an inordinate pride in her
achievements, even in a toilet free from stains and smells."[14]
However, despite years of meticulous work of a woman,
she remains too hesitant, wavering and uncertain "of her
gender roles and years later, as the couple, Jaya and Mohan,
sits in silence in a dusty flat space, the freedom from daily
drudgery feels liberating for the woman:

> "There was nothing to be cleaned,
> nothing to be arranged tidied, I was free."[15]

Jaya doesn't have to scrub clean or iron the things
of the household, at least, for the next few days till the
crisis gets over at her husband's office. This new-found
freedom makes her love the bareness and the ugliness of
the place more than anything else. In the past, she had
only her maid servant Jeeja to save her from the 'hell of
drudgery'. Deshpande, in this context, suggests a different
model which would take care of the issues relating to this
gendered nature of household works:

> "...i believe ...family should be built
> not on the sacrifice of some but on the

cooperation and compromise of all its members."[16]

If a marriage is sustained by the belief that 'a husband can do no wrong' it's equally strengthened by the helplessness of a woman who can never conceive a life beyond her marital home. This lack of choices is also reflected in the denial of a woman's right to creative expression which could have given a sense of freedom to a woman away from the stifling spaces at home. Unfortunately, in the gendered spatial politics of a marital home, a man still decides what a woman should do with her free time. While Jaya feels the pressure of her husband's constant need of 'his wanting, the burden of his clinging ', she doesn't get the minimum support in her affairs. Her stories, thus, get 'hidden' in the house and, instead, it's her little prose pieces for a woman's magazine that get the male approval. If her femininity is sealed through her domestic acts then that core idea also needs to get authenticated by the men. Thus, Jaya's serious story on a man –woman relationship is dismissed by Mohan as 'scandalous' 'exhibitionist' and merely 'autobiographical'. That just leaves her with one single career option of marriage and its duties:

> "Even a worm has a hole; it can crawl into; I had mine-as Mohan's wife, as Rahul's and Rati's mother."[17]

Within this spatial constraint and fixed marital identity, Jaya is, thus, allowed to write "light humorous pieces about the travails of a middle class housewife which are never serious at all"

In a patriarchal society, a man's right over a woman also results in his control over her space and privacy. This spatial constraint is evident in the novel as Mohan decides to give his wife a new name post-marriage. Jaya thus gets a new name and takes on a new identity:

> "Suhasini … a soft, smiling placid motherly woman. A woman who lovingly nurtured her family. A woman who coped."[18]

Jaya over a period of time gets transformed into a 'soft placid' woman as she went about maneuvering the spatial limitations of her marital home. The male urge to control the home space is also evident when Mohan meticulously erases all the traces of his wife's parental memories. Thus, all the old photographs of Jaya's people get taken off the walls and this erasure appears as an invasion into her privacy which she likens it to an "an army taking possession of invaded territory".[19]

This invasion into a woman's privacy takes an inevitable yet predictable turn when her body gets involved. Susan Bordo has confirmed that body is "a practical …locus of social control".[20] Again. Foucault's idea of a 'docile body' also refers to a body oppressed by the norms of dominant socio-cultural life. Together they suggest that a female body is at the receiving end of male identity, wishes and expectations. In Deshpande's novel, the normative values of a patriarchal home means Jaya has to do Mohan's bidding, leaving her cold at the end. Their 'silent, wordless lovemaking' is thus a routine act:

> "God, how terrible it was to know a man so well. I could time it, almost to the second, the whole process of our lovemaking, from the first devious wooing to the moment he turned away from me, offering me his hunched back".[21]

Infact, Jaya's coldest 'sensual memories' confirm more than anything else her 'aloneness'.

In *That Long Silence*, Deshpande presents a couple in the middle of a material crisis which disturbs the status quo in the marital relationship. In the process, Jaya realizes how within the home space she has been a severely curtailed being on a tight leash. Her husband, children and relatives get their interests taken care of but her 'silence' is not a defeat at the end. She, at least, doesn't have any illusion relating to her subservient state.R.S. Rajan believes this deliberate silence can be subversive too:

> "Silence as withheld communication produces mystery and enigma; it expresses displeasure: it retains secrets; it demonstrates self-discipline or resistance ..." [22]

This is precisely what Jaya does too in Deshpande's novel. By refusing to explain she retains a kind of calmness of mind: "It was so much simpler to say nothing. So much less complicated." At the same time, she takes charge of her own life as well as her body. Her decision to go for an abortion, in this context, becomes a marker of that freedom of choice. On the other hand, she decides to give her relationship another chance and this time around, she is more aware, confident and ready to negotiate the power relationships with her family members inside a marital home:

> "I will have to speak, to listen. I will have to erase the silence between us ...life has always to be made possible". [23]

NOTES

1. Blunt Alison & Dowling Robyn, Home, Routledge, U.S.A., 2006, p.3

2. Somerville Peter, Homelessness and the meaning of Home: Rooflessness or the Rootlessness?, International journal of Urban and regional research 16(4):529-539, December 1992.

3. Schissel Wendy (ed.), Home/Bodies: Geographies of Self, Place and Space, University of Calgary Press, Canada, 2006, p.4.

4. Young Marion, Intersecting voices, dilemmas of gender, political philosophy and policy, Princeton University Press, New York, 1997, p.148.

5. ibid., p. 148.

6. Chandra Singh Gitanjali, Indian women of the House of Fiction, Zubaan, New Delhi, 2008, p.27.

7. Deshpande Shashi, That Long Silence, Penguin, 1989, New Delhi, p.3.

8. ibid., p.93.

9. Massey D., A Global Sense of place, Marxism Today, June,:24-9, 1991.

10. Deshpande Shashi, That Long Silence, Penguin, 1989, New Delhi, p.30.

11. ibid., p.12.

12. Hayden Dolores, Redesigning the American dream, The future of Housing, work and family life, W.W. Norton, new York, 2002. P.84.

13. Chatterjee Partha, The Nation and its Fragments: Colonial and Postcolonial Histories, Delhi, Oxford University Press, 1994, p.120.

14. Deshpande Shashi, That Long Silence, Penguin, 1989, New Delhi, p.13.

15. ibid., p.25.

16. Deshpande Shashi, *Writing from the Margin* from Writing from the Margin and other Essays, Penguin, Viking, New Delhi, 2003, P.84.

17. Deshpande Shashi, That Long Silence, Penguin, 1989, New Delhi, p.148.

18. ibid., p.15-16.

19. ibid., p.46.

20. Bordo Susan, quoted in Meenakshi Thapan, Images of the Body and Sexuality in Women's Narratives on Oppression in the Home, Economic and Political Weekly, Vol. 30, No. 43 (Oct. 28, 1995), p. 72.

21. Deshpande Shashi, That Long Silence, Penguin, 1989, New Delhi, p.85.

22. Rajan R.S. The Name of the Husband from Real and Imagined Women, Routledge, London, 1993, p.87.

23. Deshpande Shashi, That Long Silence, Penguin, 1989, New Delhi, p.192-93.

REFERENCES

Alison & Dowling Robyn, Home, Routledge, U.S.A., 2006.

Chandra Singh Gitanjali, Indian women in the House of Fiction, Zubaan, New Delhi, 2008.

Chatterjee Partha, The Nation and its Fragments: Colonial and Postcolonial Histories, Delhi, Oxford University Press, 1994.

Deshpande Shashi, That Long Silence, Penguin, 1989, New Delhi.

Deshpande Shashi, Writing from the Margin and other Essays, Penguin, Viking, New Delhi, 2003.

Hayden Dolores, Redesigning the American Dream, The future of Housing, work and family life, W.W. Norton, new York, 2002.

Rajan R.S., Real and Imagined Women, Routledge, London, 1993.

Schissel Wendy(ed.), Home/Bodies: Geographies of Self, Place and Space, University of Calgary PressCanada, 2006.

Young Marion, Intersecting voices, dilemmas of gender, political philosophy and policy, Princeton University Press, New York, 1997.

Chapter 5

Feminism and the Role of Women in the Modern World

JAYINI GHOSH
Guest Lecturer, Dept of English,
Kanchrapara College,
North 24 Parganas,
West Bengal.

Feminism as a school of criticism is fairly new and is still evolving. According to M. H. Abrams, it was around 1960s that we find feminism as a well formed discipline in Europe. However, in one way or the other, feminism made its presence felt, to the society in general and the intellectual and creative world in particular, from early years. The advent of industrialization, which led to a shift in the economy from agrarian to that of a mercantile one, and the appearance of the labour class as the major fraction of the society has brought about a lot of alterations in the life of the people. The industrialization was a result of immense scientific development. The scientific era led to unparalleled technological progress. However the world also became witness to two devastating World Wars. The age old social structure, both in the west as well as in the east, was thoroughly destabilised. The women no longer remained restricted within their domestic chores. They had to step into the outside world and start working as the bread earners for their families. First they became factory workers and then their new role as the nation's work force contributed immensely towards the economic progress of their country. Moreover as a aftermath of the World Wars the male population dwindled in size; which made it absolutely imperative for the women to perform their duties both in the domestic as well as in the outer world. Along with this new role which doubled the responsibilities of the women all they wanted was a little appreciation and the freedom to make decisions on their own. However their work went unappreciated and when it came to decision making whether on the public front or on the household matters, their voices remained unheard-of for the longest period of time. In Europe it was a time of nation building after the two World Wars. The male domain of activities which included a lot of adventures and explorations were no longer beneficial to the country. It was a time to rebuild what was destroyed due to excessive and unjust lust for power on the part of a handful of people. Thus it was time for the men to step into the domain of women's activities, because the work of nation building is in many ways parallel to taking care of the house, which was something where the women had centuries of experience. This role of the homemaker was designated to the women by the patriarchal society. However the time was such that they could not keep their women bound within the domestic world any more. The industrial revolution saw to it. Next the World Wars devoid the men of their external activities. Now they were not only denied their place in the world but were forced to take up the activities which till now were considered second grade to their own. The nineteenth and the twentieth centuries saw such upheavals in the entire human society which was hitherto unheard of. The changes happened in all aspects of human life, be it political, economic, social or even religious. This alteration was extremely severe and inevitable. However the society was not yet ready to grant women their new position and status in this new order of things. Thus feminism became such a popular school of thoughts during this period of time. It was around the end of the eighteenth century and the beginning of the nineteenth century that feminism first made its presence felt as a major school of thought in Europe. Mary Wollstonecraft was perhaps one of the earliest women to profane feminism openly and lead her life in accordance with her ideas. It was towards the beginning of the twentieth century that we have Virginia Woolf's "*A Room of One's Own*" (1928), as a classic feminist text.

Although feminism appears to be a rather recent idealism, but we should not be mistaken in thinking that the history of the woman's struggle to acquire her rightful place in the society is something new. From the very beginning of civilization women have been denied an equal status and opportunity as accorded to the men. They are always relegated to the second place irrespective of their talent. The patriarchal society finds a woman too illogical and emotional to be in any decision making position and too sentimental to be a good creative artist. A creative woman is considered to be 'the mad woman in the attic', while an ambitious woman like Lady Macbeth is seen as the 'fourth witch'. When such women are given a psychological treatment by the authors, it is always from the point of view of a man. The women are not only denied a voice of their own but are also not allowed to have a perspective to represent their experiences and the way the world appears to them. Feminism not only seeks to fight the social injustices faced by a woman, but also tries to give a voice to her so that she can tell her story to the whole world from her own point of view, without the fear of being considered mentally ill.

Feminism like most of the other schools of criticism is not a rebellion against an existing ideology, as was the case of neo-classicism against the previous age of sentimentality or romanticism which in turn challenged the extreme logicality of neo-classicism. Feminism is trying to voice the saga of the age old oppression faced by half of the humanity at the hands of the other half. There are various sub-schools within feminism, such as the liberal feminists, the radicals, the leftist, the French feminists, the black feminists, etc. However all of them are concerned about the oppression of the women. All of them have also concluded that women have to face double the oppression in any given scenario than her male counterpart. The society always grants a second position to the women no matter what her qualities may be. Moreover if the woman belongs to a particular community which faces exploitation by the others, then she experiences twice the atrocities; first because she is a woman and then as a member of that downtrodden community. The exponents of feminism focus on various issues which they individually or as a group find important. Sometimes they relate to their personal and local experiences and at other times they are concerned about an issue of global significance.

In literature feminism has been present for centuries in an implicit manner. Authors have been extremely conscious about how they should represent the women in their works.

The portrayal of the women seems to be particularly difficult as the question remains whether they should be presented as an ideal woman, in total conformation with the societal norms or be painted in a hue of reality, thus exploring the complex facets human nature.

Let us consider Shakespeare's famous tragedy Macbeth. In the play before the murder of Duncan, Lady Macbeth appears to be a person full of confidence. She is portrayed as a confidant of Macbeth.

'My dearest partner of greatness'
(Act I, Scene V, Line 11)

This is how Macbeth addresses her in his letter describing his encounter with the witches. She inspires him to be ambitious and encourages him to go to any lengths to achieve whatever is in stored in his destiny. Lady Macbeth initially appears as a person devoid of all emotions except for insatiable ambition. She declares:

... Hie thee hither,
That I may pour my spirits in thine ear,
And chastise with the valour of my tongue
All that impedes thee from the golden round,
Which fate and metaphysical aid doth seem
To have thee crown'd withal.
(Act I, Scene V, lines 25 to 30)

However we must remember that Macbeth had already fallen a pray to greed after listening to the witches' prophecy. Banquo, on the other hand remained calm and did not give into the provocation offered by the unnatural.

We should also keep in mind that Lady Macbeth's weapon is her tongue, unlike Macbeth who is a competent general. Both Macbeth and Lady Macbeth are ambitious but Lady Macbeth can fulfil her aspirations only through Macbeth. It is therefore that she presses her husband so heard to commit regicide and take what fate has destined for both of them. It is however interesting to see how Macbeth becomes self sufficient once the deed of regicide has been committed. He no longer treats Lady Macbeth as his partner. She looses her stronghold over Macbeth. Thus the coronation of Macbeth as the all powerful king, marks the total lose of power by Lady Macbeth. We hardly see them together any more, let alone deciding on their next move. This is in a way how the patriarchy treats the women. The woman's help is frequently sought for, but once the purpose is served they are relegated to an insignificant position. The over ambitious man is accepted as the hero of a great tragedy, while the ambitious woman is tagged as a witch living within the civilized society and creating havoc. She has to suffer from madness and die as a fragile, broken hearted person. Lady Macbeth had once invoked the spirits of darkness thus:

> … Come, you Spirits
> That tend on mortal thoughts, unsex me here,
> And fill me, from the crown to the toe, top-full
> Of direct cruelty! Make thick my blood,
> Stop up the access and passage to remorse;
> That no compunctious visitings of Nature
> Shake my purpose, nor keep peace between
> Th'effect and it! Come to my woman's breasts,
> And take my milk for gall, you muth'ring ministers,

Wherever in your sightless substances
You wait on Nature's mischief! Come, thick Night,
And pall thee in the dunnest smoke of Hell,
That my keen knife see not the wound it makes,
Nor Heaven peep through the blanket of the dark,
To cry, 'Hold, hold!'
(Act I, Scene V, Lines 40 to 54)

The same person in Act V appears in a completely different light. Now she is sleep walking and speaking to herself.

The Thane of Fife had a wife: where is she
Now?
(Act V, Scene I, Lines 40 to 41)

Even through her madness we find out that for quite some time now she is no longer in aid with Macbeth. The crime of murdering Lady Macduff and her son was all Macbeth's doing. Many critics believe that regicide is a common action in power politics. However killing of the son or a son-figure is unheard of and yet Macbeth sanctions the murder of two such young boys without any provocation from Lady Macbeth. These two boys are Banquo's son who manages to escape From Macbeth's clutches and the other is young Macduff who is killed in his own palace, before his mother's eyes. Lady Macbeth had once invoked the spirits of cruelty to make her more powerful, but Macbeth commits these crimes naturally.

The most stunning fact is how these two characters are treated by the playwright. Both of them are ambitious. They together stoop to the lowest level of immorality when they murdered king Duncan, because at that point of time he was their guest. Macbeth also commissioned the killing of two young boys who could very well had been his sons. In spite of all these Macbeth gets a chance to redeem himself. Towards the very end we again see the same military general fighting for his honour. We remember Macbeth as a fallen hero who suffers from error of judgement. However Lady Macbeth is given no second chance. We don't see her regain her confident self again. She does not get the chance to fight for her glory and honour. Her actions are marked as sins for which she is doomed for eternity. She is denied the opportunity to become a tragic hero.

This discrimination on the part of the authors is perhaps even more prominent in the works of some of the later iconic writers. All of us are well aware of the storyline of Jane Eyre by Charlotte Bronte, where Mrs Bertha Antoinetta Rochester (née Mason), originally from Jamaica, spends her life in captivity in the attic under the pretext of madness. In Jamaica she was alright because Mr Rochester had married her. But as soon as Bertha Mason's purpose in Mr Rochester's life was over, she became a liability. Rochester could not send her back to Jamaica, so she is imprisoned in the attic and kept away from the sight of the people. Her sickness is at times blamed on her tropical origin. She is considered to be a whimsical person with a quick temper. Interestingly in a mystery story by Sir Arthur Conan Doyle The Problem Of The Thor Bridge, the perpetrator was a woman named Lady Maria Gibson, originally from Brazil. Here too the lady finds out about her husband, Neil Gibson's affair with her children's governess Grace Dunbar. She commits suicide in such a manner that it seemed that it was Grace Dunbar who has murdered her.

Grace was imprisoned for the crime of killing Lady Maria Gibson when Sherlock Holmes unravelled the mystery. At the end of this story both Sherlock Holmes and Dr Watson give their blessing to the relationship of Neil Gibson and Grace Dunbar. However no body seemed to be a list troubled by the fact that a woman had committed suicide due to her husband's betrayal of her. She is portrayed as a conniving woman whose actions are whimsical and irrational because of her exotic upbringing. In both these incidents the matches are found to be unsuitable because it is the husbands who change after their marriage. Both Rochester and Neil Gibson had gone to the tropical countries and taken a wife knowing fully well about their nature and culture. It was through the wife's connection that they gain in wealth and status. Then they decide to return back to Europe without any considerations for their wives wellbeing. In England both the husbands are somehow ashamed of their respective first marriages. While Rochester locks up his wife, Neil Gibson openly engages in an affair with the governess of his children. Maria not only had to face the humiliation of her husband's behaviour but that too with a woman whom she had trusted her children with. Neil Gibson and Grace would erase even her memories from her children's mind. People live on through their progeny but Maria is denied even that.

Now if we take a look into an ancient Indian text, The Mahabharata then we will find that all the characters are extremely complicated and intriguing. Draupadi is perhaps the most bold and one of the strongest characters to be found in world literature. She is married to five brothers at once. She is the empress of united India, and it was apparently for her honour that the battle of Kurukshtra was fought. According to the social norms Draupadi can be regarded as a deviant. The character of Subhadra works as a foil to Draupadi. The very name Subhadra symbolizes 'a good woman'. She is in total conformation with the societal ideologies. In a patriarchy the identity of a person is decided through his/her father. However in The Mahabharata we see that it is ultimately Subhadra's lineage that sits on the throne of Hastinapur, and not Draupadi's sons. Here it was no longer important that Draupadi's eldest son was also the child of Yaudhisthir. The society was not ready to accept Draupadi's progenitor as the ruler of their land and fate. It is for this reason that as a poetic resolution all the five sons of Draupadi and the single son of Subhadra, Abhimanyu dies in the battle; and we have Abhimanyu son Parikshit sitting on the throne after Yaudhisthir.

The most intriguing question is if these different women characters are not acceptable to the society, then why do we have them in our literature? The creative writers are sensitive individuals. They are aware of the oppression faced by the women. At times they voice their protest explicitly, but most of the times they are subtle about their points of view. In Sir Arthur Conan Doyle's *The Problem of the Thor Bridge*, Lady Maria Gibson's intelligence is matched by none other than that of Sherlock Holmes. In the Macbeth, Shakespeare has raised various issues regarding the position of a woman, her ambitions and how far can she go to achieve her desires. In the Indian society Subhadra is treated as a goddess, but in The Mahabharata there is no one like Draupadi. Her position is unparalleled in world literature.

It seems that the authors are in a state of indecision as to whether they should punish these exceptional women characters or praise them openly. To begin with these characters are given a proper treatment by the writers, but then they are as if forsaken in the mid way. May be our society and the norms followed by us are working as a deterrent in this matter. It is high time that we reform our outlook towards women and stop being blindly judgemental towards them. The advent of feminism has brought about a lot of changes in the life of the women, but there is more that needs to be done. Women should be accepted for who they are and not necessarily how much they conform to the age old orthodox points of view of the patriarchal society. Today we have stepped well into the twenty –first century. If still we set up centuries old regulations for half of the humanity then how can we make proper progress in any walk of life? Acceptance and sensitivity are the best ways to achieve our goals. Compassion is one of the greatest human virtues. If the society grants their women the rightful position and freedom to lead their life in their own terms, then it will benefit the entire humanity. One person's liberty need not curtail another person's progress. However if both the men and the women are not truly liberated then no one will be able to prosper to the fullest. It is high time that feminism not only remains bound in academic syllabus but becomes a part of the life of the common people and helps them to lose their inhibitions in allowing the women the respect and appreciation long due to them.

BIBLIOGRAPHY

Abrams, M. H. A Glossary of Literary Terms. 1999. Singapore: Thomson Asia Pte Ltd, 2004

Ahmed, Aijaz. In Theory. 1992. Delhi: Oxford University Press, 1994.

Bhabha, Homi K. The Location of Culture. 1994. New York: Routledge Classics, 2004.

Bronte, Charlotte. Jane Eyre. 1847. Ware, Hertfordshire: Wordsworth Classics, 1992.

Butler, Judith. Gender Trouble :Feminism and the Subversion of Identity. 1990. London and New York: Routledge, 1999.

Doyle, Sir Arthur Conan. The Case-Book of Sherlock Holmes. 1927. United Kingdom: John Murray, 1984.

Shakespeare, William. Macbeth. Ed. Kenneth Muir. 1951. Surrey: Thomas Nelson &Sons Ltd, 1999.

Chapter 6

Question of Women's Position in India-From History to Constitution

NIRMAL KR. SAHOO
(Asst.Prof.in Pol. Sc.) and TIC S.F.S. Mahavidyalaya
(University of Burdwan) Khayrasole,
Birbhum, West Bengal
&
TUHIN KUMAR DAS**
Asst. Prof. in Pol.Sc
Dinabandhu Mahavidyalaya
Bongaon, North 24 Pgs, West Bengal
(****Author for Corresponding**,
E-mail: hellotiash2012@gmail.com)

The issue of women is one of the most challenging and alarming issues in today's changed global context, not because they are well protected and well secured but because they are more and more battered and tortured day by day. The evidence is clear everywhere that the voice of women is being increasingly heard in the streets, courts and Parliaments, and even largely displayed in daily media. Yet issues concerning women are not given priority in society. Women always constitute an important segment of any kind of society, be it primitive or modern, agricultural or industrial. Thus, an analysis of the role of women in society throws light on the complex problem of their participation in different aspects of life. Of all the aspects of relationship between women and society, it is women's participation in various fields like social, political, educational, economic and so on that has received the most sustained attention from the social thinkers, human rights' activists and political scientists.

STATUS OF WOMEN IN INDIA

India is known for her specific culture. There is no direct reference to the notion of rights in India. However, it lies embedded in its culture. The notion of Purusharthas: Dharma (rules and regulations), Artha (material prosperity), Kama (sexual pleasure) and Moksha (eternal bliss) reflects four values of life for human development. It seeks to achieve both empirical and spiritual development of indviduals. The Vedic sages also emphasize on the development and happiness of entire humanity: "Sarve Bhavantu Sukhina" or "Let all be happy." However, one can not overlook the plethora of social evils like intolerant casteism, Sati (Burning widow while living), female infanticide, child marriage, religious orthodoxy, communalism etc. which viciated the society and blatantly violated human rights.[1]

However, it is necessary to understand the socio-political movement in India because these movements have had a great impact on the women's life in India. At the dawn of Indian history, the Vedic women possessed high status, an equal partner with men.[2] This soon became legendary and the women were sinking deeper in economic dependence, religious taboos and social subservience and were treated as second class mortals.

A steady deterioration of the status of women further reached a new low after the disruption of the Mughal Empire and the consequent political and social confusion in the 18th century. So, when the British Period started, the position of the women was, in a sense worst, in the history of India. Child marriage was almost universal among the high caste Hindus, and had ever spread to some sections of the Muslims. The practice of 'Sati' was existant and literacy among women was regarded as a source of moral danger.

With the above existing situation one of the remarkable features of modern India has been the unprecedented awakening of Indian women during the 19th and early 20th centuries. A number of movements both religious and social were launched in the middle of the 19th century, reforming Hinduism and the Indian society.[3]

The most remembered social reformer of the 19th century was Raja Ram Mohan Roy. He established the 'Brahmo Samaj' which worked earnestly for the welfare of women. Freedom and equality of women and widow remarriage were the focus of the Samaj. The cruel system of 'Sati' was abolished by the efforts of Ram Mohan Roy. The spiritual succession of Ram Mohan Roy was Keshav Chandra Sen, who popularized Brahmo Samaj and fought for women's education and even established a school for girls. It was his courage and perseverance that brought Civil Marriage Act. III of 1872 which included abolition of child marriage, permission for widow remarriage and inter- caste marriage.

A parallel religious reform movement in the form of Parthana Samaj was started by Justice Mahadeo Govind

Ranade in Poona. Swami Dayananda Saraswati founded the Arya Samaj, whose main objective was "to give equal opportunities to all persons, men and women; to acquire knowledge and to qualify themselves for whatever position in life they would like to fill".

Another eminent person who stands out is Ishwar Chandra Vidyasagar. His notable reforms are education for women and widow remarriage. Later on, in the 19th century, came the eminent liberal, Gopal Krishna Gokhale. His Bill for universal compulsory primary education brought in a fresh breeze of reform for Indian women.

The factor which contributed towards developing women's movement was the spontaneous and massive participation of women in the struggle for National Freedom. The movement as developed by Mahatma Gandhi encouraged women to participate actively in it. This participation helped in the removal of social shackles and activated women to press for political equality and in 1917 Indian National Congress elected a woman President Annie Besant for the first time.

The Government of India Act, 1919 did not enfranchise women, but it did empower provincial legislatures to remove the sex barriers at their discretion. Madras was the first Province to grant limited franchise to women in 1921, followed by other Provinces. In the first election in 1926, the Act enfranchised less than one per cent of the total female population. The vote was a symbol of equality and women wanted it.

In 1927, the All India Women's Conference was established whose emphasis was on education. But later in the wake of the new Constitution to be framed for India, the Conference also included in its function, to discuss and contribute to all questions and matters that affect the welfare of the people of India with particular reference to women and children.[4]

In 1931, the women's organizations submitted a combined memorandum before the franchise sub-committee of the Round Table Conference that was to be held in London which emphasized on: (a) Equal rights and obligations for all citizens without any bar on account of sex; (b) No disability to attach to any citizen by reason of his or her religion, caste, creed or sex, with regard to public employment, office or power of honour and in the exercise of any trade; (c) Women to fight elections; and (d) No reservation of seats for women as such nor special nominations.[5]

The Women's Conference agitated in 1934 for the appointment of a Commission on the legal disabilities of Indian women, particularly those of Hindu women with respect to inheritance and after divorce. The Government of India Act of 1935 extended the franchise and after 12 years of struggle by the women's associations, the Hindu Law Reforms Committee was appointed in 1946.

Thus, the social reformers of the 19th and early 20th centuries prepared a fertile ground on which Gandhiji could sow the seeds of inspiration for women's participation in the political movement. This participation in the freedom struggle in a true sense, was a beginning of breaking the chains of a home-bound and constructed life for Indian womanhood.

With the attainment of Indian Independence on August 15, 1947 and the framing of its Constitution, many of the demands of the women's movement were incorporated. This special attention given to the problems of women and the recognition of political equality was a radical departure from the norms prevailing in traditional India. The Indian Constitution is described as a manifesto of social revolution. But even after 63 years of its enforcement, freedom and social justice have not reached all women in the country. There is clear evidence of growing violence regarding women's rape, wife battering, family violence, dowry deaths and prostitution. This is the stark reality for millions of women. The declining value of women is surfacing in almost every aspect of life even today.[6]

CONSTITUTIONAL SAFEGUARDS FOR WOMEN'S POLITICAL UPLIFTMENT

Indian Constitution prescribes certain special provisions in favour of women's empowerment. These provisions became highlighted only in 73rd & 74th Amendment Act, 1992 when the Constitution provided thirty three percent reservation of seats to women in Panchayati Raj Institutions & Municipalities to make them equal with that of their men counterparts in the political field. Those Provisions are:

(i) Not less than one third of the seats meant for direct election of members at each tier of Panchayats & Municipalities are to be reserved for the women;

(ii) Not less than one third of the total number of seats reserved under clause (i) shall be reserved for women belonging to the Scheduled Castes or as the case may be the Scheduled Tribes;

(iii) Not less than one-third (including the number of seats reserved for women belonging to the Scheduled Castes and Scheduled Tribes) of the total number of seats to be filled by direct election in every Panchayat shall be reserved for women and such seats may be allotted by rotation to different Constituencies in a Panchayat;

(iv) Not less than one-third of the seats of Chairpersons at any level reserved for women.

Article 14 guarantees equality before law and equal protection of law to all men and women within the territory of India.

Article 15 prohibits any kind of discrimination "against any citizen on grounds only of ……………..sex".

Article 15(3) empowers the state to make "any special provision for women and children".

Article 16 (1) guarantees "equality of opportunity for all citizens in matters relating to employment or appointment to any office under the state".

Article 16 (2) forbids discrimination "in respect of any employment of office under the state" on the grounds only of "religion, race, caste, sex, descent, place of birth, residence or any one of them".

The Directive Principles of State Policy enunciated in Part-IV of the Constitution, embody the major policy goals of the welfare state. Some Articles there deal with women indirectly while a few others concern women directly and have a special bearing on their status.

The Articles that concern women indirectly include: Article 38 directs the state to secure a just social, political and economic order, geared to promote the welfare of the people; Article 39 (b), (c) and (d) relate to the distribution of ownership and control of material resources of the community for the common good and protection of children and youth against exploitation; Article 40 concerns the organization of village panchayats to promote self government; Article 41 appertains the right to work, education and public assistance in cases of unemployment, old age, sickness, disablement and other types of undeserved wants; Article 43 contains provision of work, a living wage, condition of work ensuring a decent standard of life and cultural opportunities and the promotion of cottage industries; Article 45 ensures free and compulsory education for all children up to the age 14; and Article 47 relates to raising the level of nutrition and the standard of living of the people and improvement of public health.

The Articles of Directive Principles which deal with women directly and have a special bearing on their status include: Article 39(a) right to an adequate means of livelihood for men and women equally; Article 39 (d) equal pay for equal work both for men and women; Article 39 (4) protection of the health and strength of workers-men, women and children from abuse and entry into avocations unsuited to their age and strength, and Article 42 states for just and human conditions of work and maternity relief.

Article 51A(e) of the constitution of India imposes fundamental duty upon every citizen of India to renounce the practices derogatory to the dignity of women.

Finally, Article 325 and 326 introduce Universal Adult Franchise without any distinction of sex.

Thus the special attention is given to the needs and problems of women, to enable them to enjoy and exercise their constitutional equality of status. [7]

ROLE OF JUDICIARY

The judiciary all over the world has been playing a greater role in protecting the rights of women. The Indian judiciary led by the Supreme Court has exhibited a welcome judicial activism in recognizing, popularizing and enforcing these rights. Where no direct provision is prescribed, the judiciary is contributing a lot by recognizing the workmen's right. The Supreme Court in State of *Maharashtra vs. Madhukar Narain*[8]without referring to Article 21, held that even a woman of easy virtue is entitled[9] the court has consistently maintained that the offence of rape is violation of the right to privacy of the victim.

The Supreme Court in a number of cases held that right to economic empowerment of women is a human right. In *C. Masilmami Mudaliar vs. Idol of Sri Swamina Thaswami Thirukoil*[10] the Supreme Court has recognized, highlighted and conferred the right to economic empowerment of women as a fundamental right under the Constitution of India.[11]

The Supreme Court in case of *Visaka vs. State of Rajasthan*[12] laid down a number of guidelines to remedy the legislative vacuum. The broad guidelines laid down in Visaka's case have set a new trend in the protection of the human rights to dignity of working women in the country like India.

The Supreme Court in *Delhi Domestic Working Women's Forum vs. Union of India,*[13] suggested the formulation of the scheme for awarding compensation to rape victims. In this manner in *Chairman, Railway Board vs. Chandrima Dass,*[14] the Supreme Court awarded compensation of ten lakhs to an alien woman under Article 21 of the Constitution who has been a victim of rape.

At last, it is very important to mention here that for the constitutional protection of women in India, the judiciary may make it abundantly clear that the courts have played the role of catalyst in ensuring their position in an effective manner. Thus, it is crystal clear that the Constitution of India provides Directive Principles of State Policy which are fundamental in the governance of the State. These provisions provide special favour to women and direct the State to treat male and female equally.

FORMATION OF NATIONAL COMMISSION FOR WOMEN

The National Commission for Women was set up as a statutory body in January 1992 under the National Commission for Women Act, 1990 to review the constitutional and legal safeguards for the women. It consists of a Chairperson, five members and a member Secretary being nominated by the Central Government. The Commission investigates and examines all the matters relating to the safeguards provided for the women under the Constitution and other laws and recommends for the effective implementation of those safeguards for improving the conditions of the women by the Union or by any state.

It also reviews, from time to time, the existing provisions of the Constitution and other laws affecting the women and recommends amendments there of so as to suggest remedial legislative measures to meet any lacunae, inadequacies or shortcomings in such legislations.[15]

Concluding Observation:- In spite of perceptible improvement in general socio- economic conditions of women, due to efforts made after independence, the situation continues to be grim. Despite all the constitutional provisions, legislations and court rulings it is found that much benefits are not accrued to the women. Because they are not yet behaving as active citizens, their political culture is still parochial. Though the Constitution has granted women equal rights, but in practice these rights are not sufficient because their voice is hardly given any weightage in society. The state has not still been able to stop sex barriers completely. Available statistics reveals the continued neglect of female children's health and nutrition needs, their early marriage, high fertility, poverty and inadequate access to health care. In the field of education the massive dimension of the problem of female illiteracy daunts the society which limits the achievements of women in the field of employment, training, utilization of health facilities and exercise of their legal rights. Besides the Constitutional provisions and special enactments, in the country like India, women are subject to all kinds of discrimination and humiliation. It is now the right time to give proper consideration to these issues and the laws relating to them so as to implement these provisions for the proper upliftment of women in the country.

Thus, one may conclude by saying that women in India have to go a long way to attain the complete gender justice in social, political, economic, educational and cultural field. The need of the hour is: not welfare, but development; not charity, but entitlement; not assistance, but empowerment; not structural adjustment, but structural change; not even social security but social & gender justice, if the women are to survive and flourish in the given situation.[16]

SELECTED REFERENCES

1. Soni, Suresh Kumar, *"Human Rights- Concept, Issues and Emerging Problems"* (ed.vol.), Regal Pub., New Delhi, 2007, P.22

2. Pore, Kumud, "Women and Social Reform Movements in India" in "Social Reform Movements in India: A Historical Perspective", Ed. By V.D. Divakar, Popular Prakashan, Bombay, 1991, p.104.

3. Paul, Wilkinson, *"Social Movement"*, London, Macmilan, 1971, p.11.

4. Bakshi, Rajni, *"The women's Movement in India: A Historical Perspective"*, Lokayan Publications, Delhi, 1985.

5. Mahamandal, Bharat Stree, *"Women's Indian Association and All India Women's Conference".*

6. Vidya, K. C., *"Political Empowerment of Women at the Grassroots"*, Kanishka Publishers, New Delhi, 1977, p.8.

7. Boxi, Upendra, *"Constitutional Provisions Relating to Status of Women: An Analytical Examination"*, Paper prepared for the committee on the status of women in India, 1974.

8. AIR 1991 SC 207.

9. AIR 1996 SC 1393.

10. AIR 1996 SC 1696.

11. Ibid.

12. AIR 1996 SC 1697.

13. (1995) 1 SCC 14.

14. AIR 200 SC 988, p.997.

15. Mathews, Jojo & Gautam, Manish K., *Indian Polity and Constitution"*(Comp. Wizard for IAS/PCS), ALS Pub., New Delhi, 2006, p.268.

16. Soni, Suresh Kumar,(Eds.)," *Human Rights- Concept, Issues and Emerging Problems",* Regal Pub., New Delhi, 2007, p.57.

Chapter 7

Invisible Fence of Gender Division set up by Prospero, an Erudite Magician in Shakespeare's *The Tempest*

SUBRATA HALDER
Assistant Professor of English
Sivnath Sastri College
Gariahat Road, Kolkata
Subratahaler7878@gmail.com

The Tempest is one of the famous plays of William Shakespeare. The exact date when he wrote this play cannot be found. This pay was written between 1603 and 1613. This play was written in the fourth period of his writing career. During the time of Shakespeare, Queen Elizabeth was on the throne. That time became the age of matriarchy not patriarchy. The Elizabethan age, as we see now, was the temporary age of matriarchy. But that time may be considered the occasional happy episode for the women in the age old drama of pain and pangs. After reading The Tempest we can conceive the idea through the presentation of Miranda on the stage. At the first glimpse, Miranda seems to us that she was given a unique position in the drama as she is the only concrete female character presented on the stage because when the play was written, the women were avoided for taking roles like the role of Miranda. There are three other women – Miranda's mother, Alonso's daughter and the mother of Sycorax- have been presented only on abstract level on Prospero's idealist desert island.

When Prospero was banished after his dukedom having been usurped by his own cruel brother Antonio, his daughter (not the mother of her daughter, as she was already dead) was with him and the old lord Gonzalo's helping hands delivered him some important books, on which Prospero gave more importance than his kingdom. At that moment his daughter was nothing but his cherubin-

> "Oh, a cherubin
> Thou wast that did preserve me. Thou didst smile
> Infused with a fortitude from heaven,
> When I have decked the sea with drops full salt,
> Under my burthen groaned; which raised in me
> An undergoing stomach to bear up
> Against what should ensue."

But the surprising matter is that the hands of Prospero do not shake to hold the baton against the cherubin like daughter to maintain the power of patriarchy.

From the opening to the end of the play, we see that Miranda is nothing but a mere puppet daughter in the hands of her father. She is completely controlled and dominated by her father. She does whatever her father wants. When Prospero narrates Miranda about his lost kingdom at Milan, Miranda was asked to "obey and be attentive" (I.ii, 38) without any diversion of minds while he was talking. Again and again she was reminded to be attentive by asking "Dost thou attend me?", "Dost thou hear?". Again many imperative sentences like "sit down" or "pluck my magic rob from me" were used without any hesitation to control her daughter. I think every daughter can be controlled by love in heart not by the commanding attitude of Colonel General of an army to the control the soldier.

Miranda is completely paralysed against her father. She knows well that her father is enough powerful with his extra power of magic to control her. She has been presented on the stage as cartoon of Barbie doll which is presented as moving character on the T.V. screen as the wish of graphics designer with whom Prospero may be compared. Most of the time Miranda was in sleep. She can do nothing but sleep as if she is addicted of taking sleeping pills. But the fault is not of Miranda. Rather it is the fault of her strong father who is always conscious of maintaining patriarchal order by make her sleep with his magic spell. It is well-known to Prospero that Miranda "canst not choose without sleeping".

We know that some prisoners are kept in a lonely cell in a correctional home. But why they are kept in so condition. That, to give them extra punishment and not to get the company of other prisoner is the answer. It is also done to make them understand how strong the judicial system can be against a criminal. Similarly to my opinion it was done so with the beautiful girl Miranda. To make her powerless and to show the power of a father, Prospero has kept her separated from the mainstream of the society. He, no doubt, is powerful enough as we see how he easily can raise a storm without casualty to any person. He is powerful with his magical power. We can see the whole action of the play is governed by magic. Practically every event which is important in the play is the fruit of Prospero's magic power. The storm and the supposed shipwreck, the rescue of the passengers and their being scattered in different groups on the island, the ship being safely brought ashore with the sailors sent to sleep, the coming together of Ferdinand and Miranda, the defeat of conspiracy of Antonio and Sebastian, the foiling of Caliban's intrigue, the strange banquet and its disappearance, the songs and music of Ariel, the masque of Juno, the teasing and tormenting of Caliban by the spirits- all these are done with the help of magic. Generally a father can do anything to bring happiness in the mind of his daughter or son. Prospero loved his daughter undoubtedly. But I think his love for his daughter was not unmixed rather alloyed. If he had real love for her, he may leave her to a locality i.e. the mainstream of the society where she would be happier than her present situation, because man is a social being. Rather without thinking about this he has left her isolated like a lagoon. Miranda is a lonely figure. She had no companion except Caliban but actually he was a monster- half-human and half beast. When she became adult, she met Ferdinand but it happened due to the will of Prospero. Here I can quote few words of Ania Loomba, a critic-

> "Miranda is ordered to sleep, a wake, come on, see, speak, be quiet, obey be silent and be mute?

I think she has no value at all in society and no value also to her father. Her condition is like of a statue cut in alabaster. She simply surrenders herself to the control and domination of her father.

We all know that knowledge is power. Prospero had much knowledge which he gained bit by bit through his study of magical books which he loved more than his dukedom as it is already stated earlier. We can easily assume that the books are like his bone and blood which are the symbols of power or strength of a human body. According to Caliban without books he is like a 'sable sod'-

"Without them/ He's but a sod."

The fact that he has become the slave of Prospero and he knows what is the source of his power- the power comes from his books. But about his power which he achieved through knowledge, there is no scope of any question. After having gained knowledge i.e. power, he does not sit silently. He tries to utilize his power over whom he can. In case of schooling of Miranda, Prospero tries to impose his knowledge on Miranda. He tries to teach his daughter in which way he wants. He is the one and only teacher of Miranda. He says to Miranda-

"Here in this island
We arrived and here
Gave I, thy schoolmaster made thee more profit
Than other princess (I, II 171-3).

His student i.e. his daughter was very obedient like a first bench girl. She never disobeyed the teacher i.e. her father. Ania Loomba says that Prosper has schooled her to obedience. She never raised her voice like a nagging woman or like a haughty last bench who is generally insincere and studious. She abides with her teacher very smoothly.

Actually she was chosen to have no question as her gender identity is female. To the eyes of a male, a female must not have the power to raise a question- she will do as per direction without any question.

In The Tempest we see that not only the action of Miranda is controlled by her father but also here sexuality is controlled by her father before her marriage. Thompson says that her sexuality must be controlled by her father before his surrender his daughter to Ferdinand, the son of Alonso. He gives a warning Ferdinand not to deflore the virginity of Miranda before marriage:

> "Virgin knot before
> All sanctimonious ceremonies." (IV. I 15-16)

To the eyes of Prospero, his daughter is something like a property. He wants to sell this property to Ferdinand and he knows well that the value and quality of his commodity lies in the purity of her body i.e. if she remains a virgin before her marriage. In general, it is acknowledged that by every male that nothing can be compared in return of virginity. For that reason Ferdinand a male person questions Miranda whether she is virgin or not before making her the queen of Naples-

> "I will make you
> The queen of Naples" (I.II 448-449).
> Her bright future is determined by her chastity.

Here I can raise a question. The question of male virginity is not questioned for a single time in the male dominated society. A male may make physical relationship with any woman before marriage and to the eyes of male dominated society it seems to us that it is not faulty. But if the virginity of a female is lost (either by willingly or forcefully in case of rape), a male does not want to accept her. If we go the novel Tess of the D'Urbervilles of Thomas Hardy, we shall see that Angel Clare on the wedding night forsakes Tess when she confesses him that she was raped or seduced by Alec D'Urbervilles. But she was raped not willingly or did not willingly take participation in sexual game. But it was not the fault of her. Anyhow she is deserted thought she tried to convey this sad incident of her life before marriage. Angel did not pay any heed to the request of Tess. On the other hand, he is guiltier about this case. That he made a sexual relationship with an elderly woman in London. But the surprising matter is that it was never considered faulty as he is a male. He is an evil person in the disguise of an angel. What we see his fault was not criticized by Thomas Hardy because he, being a male writer, wrote for the male and not for the female.

In the patriarchal society, every male thinks every female being is non-virtuous. In The Tempest Prospero's generalization of every woman as non-virtuous can easily be guessed in his comment

> "Thy mother was a piece of virtue, and
> She said thou was my daughter.(I.I 56-57)
> When Miranda asks "Sir, are you not my father?"

From the opinion of Prospero we can get the idea that he was doubtful about the character of his wife. In the unconscious mind, he had the doubt about the character of his wife. Even Prospero holds a low opinion about the character of the mother of Caliban. He calls Sycorax a "wicked dam" and hates Caliban very much:

"Thou poisonous slave, got by the devil himself
Upon thy wicked dam (I.II 320)

Again the power of patriarchy does not allow him consider Sycorax a normal woman. He considers her a black wicked witch. He calls her a foul witch, a damned witch and a hag. A question may be thrown here whether Prospero used any kind of slang languages for the usurper of his kingdom i.e. his won brother Antonio and the king of Naples i.e. Alonso. I think that this is a rhetorical question as the answer can easily be expected from a misogynist Prospero. Really he has not used any sort of slang language for those male persons. His verdict of using slang language is partial as he is a male who sees a male and a female each with his different eyes. He can easily throw without any hesitation to a female sex. Sycorax was never seen by him. I think an odd anger was already reserved for her as she was a female. According to Orgel, Prospero looks upon her as the extreme negative assumptions about a woman.

Having agreed to the opinion of Ania Loomba, we can say that Prospero's anger towards Sycorax is equal to his anxiety of the woman in power i.e. Sycorax. When Prospero calls her a witch, his anxiety about woman is actually revealed. To Prospero, Sycorax is the source of anxiety as if his sleep has been snatched away by the fear or anxiety of Sycorax.

To cover the fear or anxiety about Sycorax, the representation of female sex, Prospero uses the slang 'witch'. To Prospero, Sycorax is the representative of potential power to challenge the patriarchal power. Once upon a time in England, the term 'witch' was a very hack necked insult and this insult was not applied to any kale sex but it was applied to some female sex because they, as considered by every male, were desirous to hold the power as they did not want to be doll anymore. Total 2415 words

WORKS CITED

1. http://shakespeareglobal.blogspot.in/2011/02/miranda-chaste-silent-and-obedient.html
2. Extremes of Gender and Power: Sycorax's Absence in Shakespeare's The Tempest Brittney Blystone, Northern Kentucky University Volume V:2012
3. Ania Loomba "From Gender, Race, Renaissance Drama"
4. Stephen Orgel "Prospero's Wife" Representations 1.8 (Autumn, 1984) 1-13 JSTOR, Web. 8th March 2012
5. Phyllis Rackin, "The Places of Women in Shakespeare's World: Historical Fact and Feminist Interpretation
6. Helene Cixous" The Newly Born Woman 1975

Chapter 8

Woman, Mississippian, Narrator- Precarious Jugglery of Identities in Eudora Welty's *A Curtain of Green and Other Stories*

SUMAN BANERJEE
Ph D Research Scholar
Department of English
University of Kalyani

Literature of the American South possesses a unique and distinguishing flavor. Placing Eudora Welty (1909-2001)'s work against the backdrop of 'Southern' literature often proves to be a tricky task, the reason being summed up precisely by Louis Bogan in his article titled "The Gothic South" in the December 6th, 1941 issue of the *Nation*, which is also a review of Welty's first published collection of short stories, *A Curtain of Green and Other Stories* (1941). Probing the possible reasons behind the abundance of output in Southern "Gothic" literature, he differentiates between Faulkner and Welty, and the distinctive ways in which they handle their Southern situations and characters (*Eudora Welty: The Contemporary Reviews*, 11). Bogan praises Welty's "method which opens and widens the field and makes it more amenable to detached observation. Welty's gift of detailed observation and enlivening description, coupled with detachment of observation lend poignancy to her narratives. Particularly important is the way Welty draws in minute detail the Southern female characters, delineating between conventional and unconventional specimens. In fact the collection of Welty's stories under present discussion can be viewed as a procession of Southern women refusing to be contained within the strict bounds of conventionality, leading to charged scenarios culminating in (as the case may be) tragic instability or grotesquerie. In fact, Peter Schmidt opines that the "seventeen stories collected in Eudora Welty's first book *A Curtain of Green* are haunted by the sound of women crying, by images of disheveled hair and hidden grimaces" (*The Heart of the Story*, 4). The different stories with their myriad situations and plethora of characters are bound together by being situated in the Southern state of Mississippi, which prompts King Adkins ("Eudora Welty's Other Short Story Cycle: A Reading of *A Curtain of Green*") to look upon this collection of seventeen stories as "an example of short story cycle if for no other reason than the stories' common element of place." Our discussion regarding Welty's treatment of Southern women would hinge around three of the stories in *A Curtain of Green and Other Stories*- 'Lily Daw and the Three Ladies', 'A Piece of News' and 'Why I Live at the P.O'.

The very title of the first story in the sequence 'Lily Daw and the Three Ladies' suggests this marked delineation between Lily Daw and the 'ladies' of Victory. Lily, partially retarded and brought up by the charitable ladies of Victory, continually finds herself threatened by scandal and consequently, confinement. Lily's retarded nature and lack of maturity keep the ladies permanently on their toes, as they try to exert control over her. But Lily, by now in her teens, attempts to break free from them, as is evidenced from her talking back and visiting circuses. Such behavior is regarded as ominous by her guardians, who decide that sending her away to an asylum in Ellisville would be the only remedy. The irony of the situation when they decide to send Lily away to the asylum is aptly brought by Peter Schmidt:

> When Mrs. Carson, Mrs. Watts and Aimee Slocum hear about what happened at the circus, they realize that they have arranged just in time to entomb her permanently within propriety at the Institute for Feeble Minded at Ellisville: "Lily Daw's getting in at Ellisville," they whisper to the other women in the post office, as if she had graduated from high school and been accepted at the prestigious college of her choice.

> (*Heart of the Story*, 12)

While it is true that these were the very women who had given "all her food and kindling and every stitch she had on", besides Baptizing her and giving her a place to stay, it is obvious that Welty takes a dig at their present attitude towards Lily, trying to shape all her activities according to their lady-like standards. The narrator's presentation of views and occurrences in concurrence with the ladies' perspective heightens the effect of irony.

Lily's wide-eyed fascination for the red-haired xylophone player and her suddenly-sprung desire to get married are signals that sound an alarm to these ladies, hastening their decision to send Lily away. But looking deeper we would find that rather than the primness of these ladies, it is their husbands and their social status which lend authority to these ladies. It is marriage that lends credence to whatever they say or think. That is why Lily dares to slight the relatively poor Aimee Slocum, the only spinster among the trio of ladies. But the ladies' acting out the roles assigned to them is not always secured through strict policing by Victory's patriarchs. Rather, it is the complete infusion and internalization of patriarchal principles that lead people like Mrs. Carson to wear black all the time, or socially perform according to decorum at all times. Welty's sly digs at the imprisoning institution of marriage become perceptible in the either/or choices between Lily's going to the asylum at Ellisville and her getting married to the xylophone player. More ironic is the playing of 'Independence March' by the band gathered at the railway station to see Lily off on her journey toward the Institute for the Feeble Minded at Ellisville (*The Collected Stories of Eudora Welty*, 25). Though Lily's journey is ultimately cancelled following the xylophone player's showing up at the station and her getting married to him instead, the underlying implication that marriage for Southern women is only a gateway to a life of gloomy imprisonment is persistently carried forward as Lily wears a travelling dress made out of Mrs. Carson's "last summer's mourning" to her marriage ceremony.

So far as Welty's narrative strategy for this particular story is concerned we find the views and preferences of the ladies- Mrs. Carson, Mrs. Watts and Aimee Slocum outwardly concurring with those of Victory's patriarchs. But a thorough and careful study reveals undertones of dialogic friction between the code of conventions and the ladies' personal, feminine sensibilities. Aimee Slocum's sudden urge to get Lily off the train and get her married to the man whose undue attention towards her had hastened them to send Lily away is a paradox the story ends with. And in this activity it is neither of the married ladies but quite strangely Aimee Slocum who plays the leading role. But then, being the poor spinster that she is, in a town that values women based on their post-marital social status, Aimee would know better than her married compatriots.

The story titled 'A Piece of News' actively involves only two characters-Ruby Fisher and her husband Clyde, both from Mississippi. But the crisis in the story develops when Ruby reads a piece of news in a Tennessee newspaper about a Ruby Fisher who had been shot in the leg by her husband. Being the country bumpkin that she is, she at once starts fantasizing, almost believing for a while that the news was a prophecy about her future. While there is an unmistakably comic suggestion involving mistaken identity, a closer look into the situation provides a somber clue. The story begins with an unabashed celebration of Ruby Fisher's feminine sensuality, as she comes in partially wet from the rain, trying to warm herself by the fireside:

> She stood turning in little quarter turns to dry herself, her head bent forward and the yellow hair hanging out streaming and tangled. She was holding her skirt primly out to draw the warmth in.

Then, quite rosy, she walked over to
the table and picked up a little bundle."

(*The Collected Stories of Eudora Welty*, 26)

Though this sensuality was something which expressed
itself when she was in complete solitude, it was definitely
an inalienable part of her nature:

When she was still, there was a
passivity about her, or a deception of
passivity, that was not really passive at all.
There was something in her that never
stopped.

(*The Collected Stories of Eudora Welty*, 27)

A part of this sensual nature manifests itself when she
imagines herself as the Ruby Fisher of the news article, shot
dead and lying shrouded:

At once she was imagining herself
dying. She would have a nightgown to lie
in, and a bullet in her heart. Anyone could
tell, to see her lying there with that deep
expression about her mouth, how strange
and terrible that would be.

(*Collected Stories*, 28)

While the incongruity resulting from the imagination
of "the deep expression about her mouth" takes a dig at her

sentimentality, it nevertheless reminds us of her husband Clyde's power over her. The very fact of Ruby's imagining that Clyde may shoot her if he gets angry stems from Ruby's extreme fear of Clyde's anger and his violent nature. Even in her imagination of lying dead "with a bullet in her heart" she sees Clyde as he was when younger, handsome and strong. It is Clyde's propensity towards violence that makes her shudder, as "she stood waiting, as if she half thought that would bring him in, a gun leveled in his hand" (*Collected Stories*, 27). When Clyde finally does come in, the anger in his tone is evident:

> "You've been again, haven't you?", he
> almost chuckled. (…) "Some day I'm going
> to smack the livin' devil outa' you", he said.

While the source from where Ruby had procured the newspaper infuriates Clyde once more, as soon as he takes a look at the piece of news, he realizes it is a Tennessee newspaper, reporting the misfortune of another Ruby Fisher. However, for a moment, as they stare at each other-

> (…) they both flushed, as though with
> double shame and double pleasure. It was
> as though Clyde might really have killed
> Ruby, and as though Ruby might really
> have been dead at his hand. Rare and
> wavering, some possibility stood timidly
> like a stranger between them and made
> them hang their heads.

(*Collected Stories*, 30)

While violence does not mark the ending of the story, a much more subtle realization dawns upon Ruby- unlike her body (and its attendant sensuality, which is too much for Clyde to handle, as a consequence of which Ruby often leads her double life of afternoons spent "in the shed of the empty gin") which is unique to her, her name isn't. More so is the case with her surname, for which she is dependent on her marriage to Clyde. While in her imagined death, all she could find solace in was "the deep expression about her mouth" and Clyde stooping remorsefully over her corpse, the lack of violence on Clyde's part at the end of the story leads her with a profounder sense of nothingness at the core of her being. Outside, though the storm had passed, it had left behind "faintness like a wagon crossing a bridge" (*Collected Stories*, 31). Though faint, the force of this profounder realization that dawned upon her (similar to that which suddenly hits upon Aimee Slocum towards the end of 'Lily Daw and the Three Ladies') leaves a stronger impress. Besides, the lack of violence on this specific occasion was also like the present passing away of the storm, threatening to return with full might in the future.

Moving on to the third story from the present collection of Welty's short stories, 'Why I Live at the P.O.' we are brought to the threshold of grotesquerie. The narrative in this story is mostly in the first person, as we are held witness to proof after proof of why the narrator Sister leaves home and settles at her workplace, the local post office at the end of the story. In 'Lily Daw and the Three Ladies', Welty had cleverly subverted patriarchy by assuming the narrative perspective of the respectable ladies of Victory, sufficiently indoctrinated to uphold patriarchal conventionality through their conduct. In 'Why I Live at the P.O.' the author seemingly sides with the narrator to hint at the underlying obsession that captivates the narrator's being, namely the excessive importance attached to reason. But as Charles E. May has succinctly pointed out, criticism regarding the story seems to contend itself at labeling Sister a schizophrenic, which leaves a lot out of the compass of discussion (*Eudora Welty: Bloom's Modern Critical Views*, 72).

That the stories in *A Curtain of Green* owe heavily to Welty's travels around Mississippi while working for the Works Progress Association has been stressed by many scholars and critics. So far as 'Why I Live at the P.O.' is concerned, she herself stated that once she "(…) did see a little post office with an ironing board in the back through the window", and that is probably where she received the imaginative stimulus to write to write the story. The importance of the post-office as a gathering place for local people in the South (comparable to the role of the inns and innyards in Victorian fiction) resonates through many of the stories in the collection. Sister, the narrator protagonist of the present story is an employee at the local post-office, a job which she has secured through the influence of her mother's father-Papa Daddy. It would not be unjustified to see her laying overt stress on reason as a manifestation of her confidence garnered through employment. Unlike the other women in the stories discussed-the married ladies in 'Lily Daw' or Ruby in 'A Piece of News', Sister is the chief bread-earner of the family. Her troubles start over when her younger sister Stella Rondo returns, breaking up her marriage with Mr Whitaker (whom Sister had first gone out with), with a two year old child whom she calls 'adopted'. Stella Rondo's animosity towards Sister is not confined only in winning over Mr Whitaker, but continues after her return home. Going through previous criticisms of Welty's short fiction, Charles E. May takes up R.P. Warren, who had pointed out that:

> Welty's typical fictional character is, in one way or another, isolated from the world. Around this character, (…) Eudora Welty creates either the drama of the isolated person's attempt to escape into the real world, or the drama of the discovery, either by the isolated character or by the reader, of the nature of the particular predicament. Of these two types, "Why I Live at the P.O." seems clearly to belong to the latter. Moreover, it seems equally clear that since Sister is less interested in discovering than justifying her situation, the drama of the story resides in the reader's gradual discovery of just exactly why Sister does live at the P.O.

(*Bloom's Modern Critical Views: Eudora Welty*, 65)

And it is this "gradual discovery" by the reader which opens up the possibility of a feminist reading of the story, which should properly begin from the very name 'Sister'. Her name suggests a relation (to others), not a being. The referential nature of her name suggests the incompleteness of her being, which echoes Stella Rondo's telling Mr Whitaker that Sister was "bigger on one side than the other" (*Collected Stories*, 62), both depicting her dependent

status. This dependence is not economic, unlike those of
the married ladies of Victory or that of Ruby Fisher; but
the emotional sustenance that feminine nature demands
for self expression is stifled and misrepresented through
such instances of "calculated falsehood" by Stella Rondo,
or forcefully demolished by the likes of Uncle Rondo, who
throws crackers into Sister's room early in the morning.
While Sister's persistent attempt to rationalize her decision
of leaving home and taking shelter in her workplace may
seem "a terrifying case of dementia praecox", it is Welty's
subtle skill which hints at the causal connections lying
hidden underneath. And the roots of Sister's predicaments
lay less in brutish male behavior and more in female
collaboration with their norms. It is worthless discussing
whether Sister's argument that her mother wouldn't have
extended the same warm welcome to her (if she like Stella
Rondo had run away with got married and later returned
with a two year old child) would be true or not. But after
the altercations (instigated by Stella Rondo, as Sister claims)
with first Papa Daddy and then Uncle Rondo, Sister tries
to point out clearly how her words have been contorted to
result in dispute.

Last but not the least, it must be pointed out how all
members of the Rondo family refuse to listen to others,
compulsively talking at all times. When Sister tries to
explain to Papa Daddy that she had not slighted his habit
of never shaving off his beard, Sister says that Papa Daddy
"(…) acts like he just don't hear me. Papa Daddy must
have gone stone deaf" (*Collected Stories*, 64). Again, Sister's
mother refuses to listen to her arguments when she says she
wouldn't have found the same welcome, had she done what

Stella Rondo has done. Sister herself is no different, as the last sentence of the story illustrates:

> And if Stella-Rondo should come to me this minute, on bended knees, and attempt to explain the incidents of her life with Mr. Whitaker, I'd simply put my fingers in both my ears and refuse to listen.

(Collected Stories, 73)

While excess of rationality on the part of Sister strikes the reader as a sign of her madness, the readers' task is to look beneath the pall of insanity and discover how the Mississippian female narrator's place in society is dictated by terms that cannot allow her to express herself, even though economically they are dependent on her. Her authority is challenged not in a direct way, but slyly subverted by branding her as insane.

WORKS CITED

Adkins, King. "Eudora Welty's Other Short-Story Cycle: A Reading of *A Curtain of Green.*" *South Carolina Review* Fall 42.1 (2009): 12-21. Web. 15 Sept. 2015.

Bogan, Louis. "The Gothic South" *Eudora Welty: The Contemporary Reviews.* Ed. Pearl Amelia. McHaney. Cambridge, U.K.: Cambridge University Press, 2005. 10-11. Print.

May, Charles E. "Why Sister Lives at the P.O." *Bloom's Modern Critical Views: Eudora Welty, Updated Edition.* Ed. Harold Bloom. New York: Chelsea House, 2007. 63-70. Print.

Schmidt, Peter. "The Anxiety of Authorship: Heroines and Women Artists in a *Curtain of Green.*" *The Heart of the Story: Eudora Welty's Short Fiction.* Jackson, Mississippi: University of Mississippi, 1991. 3-48. Print

Schmidt, Peter. "Rigidity and Rebirth: Eudora Welty and Women's Comedy." *The Heart of the Story: Eudora Welty's Short Fiction.* Jackson, Mississippi: University of Mississippi, 1991. 109-203. Print.

Welty, Eudora, and Peggy Whitman. Prenshaw. *Conversations with Eudora Welty.* Jackson: University of Mississippi, 1984. 161. Print.

Welty, Eudora. *The Collected Short Stories of Eudora Welty.* San Diego: Harcourt Brace Jovanovich, 1980. Print.

Chapter 9

Women writers in Prabasi, a Bengali periodical: 1901-1920

NANTU ACHARJYA
Librarian
Shyamnagar Kanti Chandra High School,
Shyamnagar, 24 Pargana (North), West Bengal

INTRODUCTION

It is said that the practice of literary work of Bengali women had started from the second half of the 19th century. Basically women education began in the 19th century. At that time the society was in transitional phase in education and litarature. In 1849 Calcutta Female School had been setup. Vidyasagar, Mr. Bethun, Madan Mohan Tarkalankar had put in great effort to establish women education. Different organizations like the Brahmho Samaj, the Hindu Samaj were also engaged with women education, women developments etc. Hindu and Brahmo women were identified through their own literary works, thoughts and ideas. In this case periodicals helped these women to express their cultural activities. In this article the famous Bengali periodical "Prabasi" has been analyzed to explore the women writer.

ABOUT PRABASI

Prabasi a Bengali journal regularly published for more
than sixty years, was started by Ramananda Chattopadhyay
(1865-1943) in Baishakh, 1308 BS (April 1901), in
Allahabad. Ramananda, having failed in his short-lived
ventures with Pradip and Dasi, brought out the monthly
Prabasi on his own. Chintamoni Ghosh, the owner of
the Indian Press at Allahabad, helped him in the venture.
Ramananda taught in a local college but resigned in 1906.
Then he simultaneously started an English monthly, the
Modern Review, from Allahabad. Within two years, the
British Government ordered him to leave Allahabad,
finding some fault with the English journal, which was
propagating Swadeshi ideals. Ramananda finally settled in
Calcutta in 1315 BS and continued to publish both the
journals from the city. Ramananda edited both of them
almost until his death. Prabasi's fame remains unsurpassed
by any other Bengali periodical during this period.

Prabasi maintained its publications with strict regularity
after the first few years. Well edited and well produced, it
contained multicolored prints of paintings from the second
year onwards. Prabasi regularly published articles on art and
artists and religiously published the works of the Bengal
School of artists, Ramananda helped much in popularizing
the works of Abanindranath Tagore, Nandalal Bose and
others. Even paintings by some European artists were first
published in Prabasi. Ramananda himself was interested
in art studies and wrote on the Ajanta Cave paintings in
the first issue. Besides the editor himself, OC Ganguly and
Sister Nivedita wrote many such articles.

Many popular and important literary work of Rabindranath Tagore were published in Prabasi almost regularly from 1314 BS, until his demise. It is no exaggeration to say that his major creations reached Bengali homes through it. Prabasi offered variety unmatched by any contemporary journal. Ramananda inspired Gnanendramohan Das to write on the Bengalis residing outside Bengal, which culminated in a two-volume study, Banger Bahire Bangali. Though creative writing was its forte, articles on history, art, archaeology, sociology, education, literature and literary theories, scientific topics, and travelogues were published regularly. The journal discussed contemporary social, economic and political issues. In a section called Vividha Prasanga (Varied Topics), Ramananda chronicled contemporary national and international events. In short, Bengali culture in the first half of the twentieth century is amply reflected in the pages of Prabasi. In the first forty years, the number of contributors to Prabasi crossed 350. Almost all major poets and prose writers of the day appeared in it, a notable exception being Sarat Chandra Chattopadhyay. No surprise that Prabasi gained unmatched popularity without lowering its dignified status. Its almost complete set is available in many libraries, but no index has yet been published.

OBJECTIVES

This paper reveals the following objectives

⇒ To identify the women writer in 1901-1920
⇒ To study the literary work of women writer

⇒ To identify the different forms of work of women
    writer in Prabasi
⇒ To study the subject areas of the articles, written
    by women

METHODOLOGY

Prabasi has a huge publication throughout its journey
(approx 60 years). For this article documents analysis
method of quantitative research has been used. The
statistical approach, content analysis etc are applied as basic
techniques. Hence the data which are related to the topic
i.e. subjects, forms, and other facets have been collected.
Then identification of the basic subject of the publication
are done and listed. In this way the facets are identified.
For this identification the Dewey Decimal Classification
(DDC) schedule 19th edition and Sears List of Subject
Headings, 19th edition have been consulted.

DATA COLLECTION AND ANALYSIS

The selected period of Prabasi journals are collected.
Various data are collected to fulfill the mentioned
objectives. MS Excel 2007 has been used for making
analysis and drawing tables and charts.

YEAR-WISE DISTRIBUTION OF PUBLICATIONS

The following bar chart shows differnt years and the publications of the women writer during these years. The starting year was 1901. Three publications were found in this year. And it is also found that the number of women writer were increased year by year. The highest number of publications were found in the year 1918 (i.e.52). It shows that the works of women writer were increasing those years.

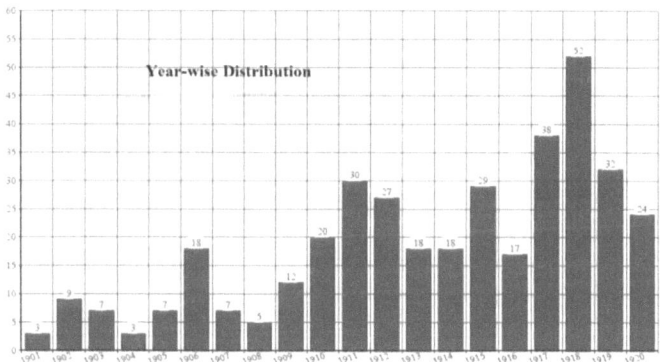

TOP 10 RANKS OF WOMEN WRITER

The following table shows top 10 ranks of the women witer according to their citations. In the time of data analysis it was found that there were 66 women writer, including eight pseudonyms, which were indicating females. Here in this table only top 10 among them have been shown. Priyambada Debi and Hemlata Debi have jointly achieved rank one (each of them has 52 citations). And the 10th position has been achieved jointly by four women for each and every one of them has 5 citations. They are Nibedita; Profullomoyi Debi; Probashini [a pseudonym] and Shoilobala Ghosh. Besides these women writer there are 50 writers left. Among them Kusum Kumar Das (Mother of Poet Jibonananda Das) and Krishna Bhabini Das were renowned.

Rank	No. of citation	Name of Women Writers
1	52	প্রিয়ম্বদা দেবী
1	52	হেমলতা দেবী
2	43	শান্তা দেবী
3	39	নিরুপমা দেবী
4	27	সীতা দেবী
5	17	লজ্জাবতী বসু
5	17	সংযুক্তা দেবী
6	9	শৈলবালা ঘোষ জায়া
7	8	অতসী দেবী
7	8	সরোজ কুমারী দেবী
8	7	অনঙ্গমোহিনী দেবী
9	6	শান্তা চট্টোপাধ্যায়
10	5	নিবেদিতা
10	5	প্রফুল্লময়ী দেবী
10	5	প্রবাসিনী
10	5	শৈলবালা ঘোষ

Table 1: Top 10 Ranks of Women writer

FORM WISE DISTRIBUTION

The following chart reveals the basic form of literary works of women writer during these period. The writings were mainly categorized into six sections, i.e. Biographies, Discussions, Essays, Novels, Poetry and Stories. Among these six sections, women writer were much comfortable with poetry. In this analysis it is found that there were 376 publications written by women from the year 1901 to 1920. Out of 376 publications, 134 publications were poems. Women were more aware of subject other than literature. There were 77 individual essays as well as articles published on different subjects.

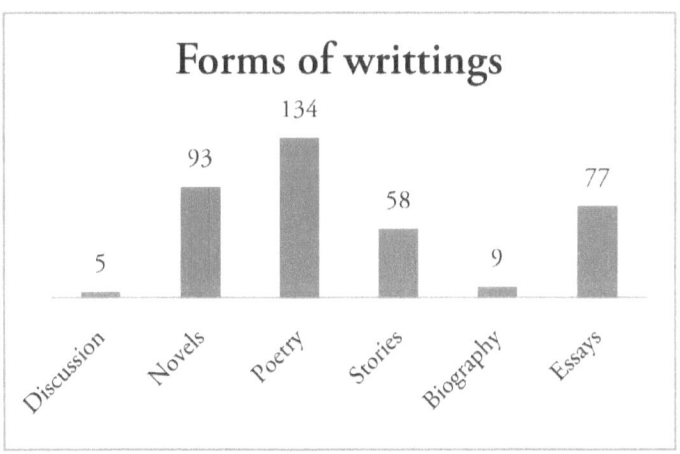

DISTRIBUTION OF NOVELS

The following table shows that thare were eight novels published during 20 years. Udyanlata was published within

17 months. It was written by Sanjukta Debi. The shortest novel was Alor Araal by Sita Debi. It was completed within three months in April, 1920 to June, 1920.

Name of Novels	No. of Citations
দিদি	16
সেথ আল্দু	11
স্মৃতির সৌরভ	10
শ্যামলী	16
উদ্যাললতা	17
সোনার থাঁচা	8
আলোর আড়াল	3
চিরন্তুলী	12
Total	93

Table 2: Names of Novels with citations

RANK OF WOMEN POET

The following table shows the ranks of the women poet according to their works. 134 poem have been identified. Outof 66 women writers, 27 women been identified as poetess in this article. Here Priyambada Debi was the most cited woman poet of this period. She composed 51 poems and achieved rank 1. Rank 2 has been achieved by Lojjaboti Bosu with 16 poetic works. She was followed by Hemlota Debi who achieved rank 3 with 15 poems. Three of them used psedonyms.

Rank	Name of Poet	Rank	Name of Poet
1	প্রিয়ম্বদা দেবী	10	অনামিকা দেবী
2	লজ্জাবতী বসু	10	আমোদিনী ঘোষ
3	হেমলতা দেবী	10	ইন্দিরা দেবী
4	অনঙ্গমোহিনী দেবী	10	জগৎমোহিনী দেবী
5	সরোজ কুমারী দেবী	10	জনৈক হিন্দু মহিলা
6	প্রফুল্লময়ী দেবী	10	নির্মলা বসু
7	ইন্দুবালা দেবী	10	বঙ্গমহিলা
7	নিরুপমা দেবী	10	লীলাবতী মিত্র
8	কুসুম কুমারী দাস	10	লজ্জাবতী দেবী
8	বিনয় কুমারী ধর	10	সরোজ কুমারী গুপ্ত
9	প্রতিভা ধর	10	সরলা দত্ত
9	শশিবালা দেবী	10	সুশীলা দেবী
9	সরযু বালা সেন	10	হিন্দু বিধবা
		10	হেমপ্রভা দত্ত

Table 3: Rank of Women poet with Number of poetry

DISTRIBUTION OF SUBJECTS OF THE ESSAYS

The following figure easily reveals the basic subjects of the essays which were writen by women writer during 1901-1920. There are 21 basic subjects been identified after analysis of the data. Here in this figure the subject 'Travel' is cited in 22 essays. 8 essays are identified with two different subjects on 'Religion' and 'Festivals' respectively.

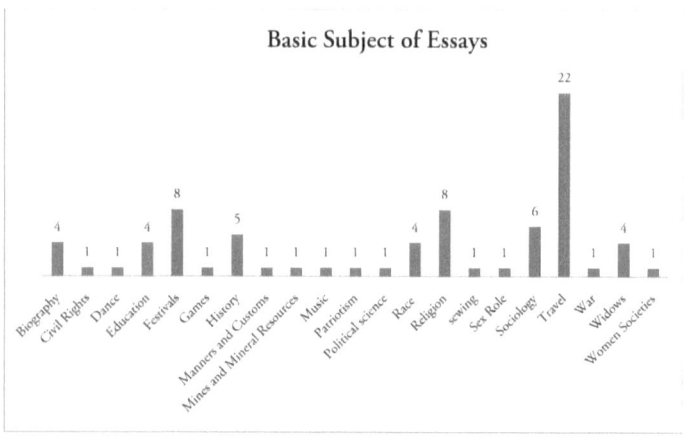

Figure 3: Basic Subjects of the Essays

FINDINGS

After analysing the data the following findings are identified

- There were 376 publications which were written by women found.
- There were 66 women writers including eight pseudonyms.
- Writings were mainly categorized into six sections, i.e. Biographies, Discussions, Essays, Novels, Poetry and Stories.
- Poetry was the most popular literary genre among women writer.
- There were 27 women poet identified
- Priyambada Debi and Hemlata Debi were the most cited writers of that period.

- The maximum publications of the women writer were found in the year 1918.
- The long cited Novel was Udyanlata by Sanjukta Debi (17th months)
- Priyambada Debi was the most cited poetess.
- The poems of Priyambada Debi were very short; most were written limited within six to eight lines. Some of these were completed within four lines as well.
- It is identified that there were 21 basic subjects covered by women writer. These are Biography; Civil Rights;Dance; Education; Festivals;Games; History; Manners and Customs; Mines and Mineral Resources; Music; Patriotism; Political science; Race; Religion; Sewing; Sex Role; Sociology; Travel; War; Widows and Women Societies.
- Maximum number of essays were written on Travel and Tour. These articles were based on their own experiences and some of the articles were about foreign countries.
- It is found that women writer did not write any essays on Physics, Chemistry, Mathematics, Biology, Technology, Philosophy, Languages and other science based theories.

CONCLUSION

Women are also a good writer, there is no doubt about it. But in the 19th century when women were subjected to supression by the society, by their family physically, mentally, educationally, politically and in many others ways. In this trying condition women had to liberate themselves. With the help of great men like Vidyasagar, Ram Mohan Roy, Rabindranath Tagore and others women education and women development took place and had succeeded. In this article it is clearly seen how the women writer were making progress in those days. They placed themselve in a strong position in the field of literature with their male counterparts.

In this article 376 publications are identified and all these publications mostly focused on womens view, womens pain, womens sorrow. Poetry, Stories, Novels were the best way to express feelings and emotions easily. Most of the poetry during this period identifies with women's pain, women's dream, women's realities and their hopes ans aspirations.The novels were based on the social condition of women, more than one marriage concept, values of women etc. Stories were also based on women's dream, their love, their thinking, their loneliness, etc. Most of the essays were written on the view point of the gender equality, the sacrifices made by women, women education, religion for women, rituals for widows, religious practice for the women, etc. Specifically in the novel Didi by Nirupama Debi, it is shown that the sacrifice, the woman made in her life is greater than man. Another Novel was Shyamali, where Shyamali, a dumb girl, fell in love with Anil, the hero. In the end Anil accepted her and cured her and set up a school for dumb children. In this story Shyamali had a strong will power. Cultural integreaty between Hindu and Muslim was the main theme of the novel called Shekh Aandhu.

Basically all the writtings of women that are found in Prabasi somehow related to their own wishes, hopes, dreams and thoughts. It has been seen that the renaissance of cultural and litarary work of women has began to flow in newer streams in the dawn of 20th century with Prabasi. Ramananda Chattopadhyay was responsible for this literary movement of women. Till his death (1943) he had tried to develop women education, women right, women status. Prabasi gave the chance to women to prove themselves as writer.

REFERENCES

- Chattopadhyay, Gita. (1990) Bangla Samoyik Patrika Ponji: 1900-1914. Calcutta: BLA
- Chowdhury, Kamala. (2004) Probasi Nirbachito Songkolon. Kolkata: Mitra O Ghosh
- Majumder, Ujjwal Kumar & Mosel, Basudeb Edited. (1997) Probasi Nirbachito Golpo Songkolon. Kolkata: Annopurna Prakashoni.
- http://en.banglapedia.org/index.php?title=Prabasi accessed on 25.06.2015

Chapter 10

Islam and Feminism: Muslim Women and Their Rights – A Reading in the Light of Traditional Scriptures

DR. BITTOO RANI
Assistant Professor
Department of Political Science
Dinabandhu Mahavidyalaya
North 24 Parganas, West Bengal

No other issue can be more regretful than the fact that Muslim women are treated as second-class citizens inspite of Islamic jurisprudential texts according them equality and justice as their male counterparts. The Principles of Islam and Sharia accord full equality of all Muslims, regardless of their gender, both in their public and private lives. A reading of the Holy Text (Quran)[1] reveal that gender

---

[1] The Quran is the primary source of law in Islam and is believed by Muslims to be the word of God revealed through the Angel Gabriel over a period of approximately 23 years. It has 6,666 verses, divided into 114 chapters and 30 parts. *ShaheenSardar Ali (ed.2006), 'Conceptualising Islamic Law, CEDAW (United Nations Convention on the Elimination of All Forms of Discrimination against Women) and Women's Human Rights in Plural Legal Settings: A Comparative Analysis of Application of CEDAW in Bangladesh, India and Pakistan,* available at

equality and social justice are intrinsic values and cardinal Principles, nevertheless, gender equality are not actualized in the lives of most Muslim women. The lives of most Muslim women, whether they be a citizen of any Islamic state or a Western state are governed and conditioned by male jurists constructions of beliefs and laws, for which divine mandate are claimed, inspite of not theirs not being so in totality.

ISLAMIC FEMINISM

Islamic feminism as a form of feminism rooted within the discourse of Islamic religion with the Quran as its central locus advocates the rights of Muslim women, their equality in gender relations and social justice.With the aim of presenting an egalitarian version of Islam, the movement thrusts upon purging all patriarchal interpretations of Islamic ideals. With the ideal of presenting more choices to Muslim women, the Islamic feminist consciousness has set itself the task of empowering themselves. However, researches have revealed that though grounded in Islam, much Islamic feminists have also relied upon non-Islamic feminist discourses (as Western and Secular) thereby integrating the movement for Muslim women rights with the integrated global feminist movement.

A groundswell of strong sentiments of Muslim women has emerged seeking to reclaim rights and claims granted by the Quran and Sunnah; they no longer are willing to

---

www.unifem.org.in.PDFcomplete%20study.pdf.pdf accessed on 19/10/2015, p. 9 (footnotes)

make a choice between their identity as Muslim women and their belief in gender equality. The choice wasindeed tough because choosing either one would amount to betraying their feminist consciousness or their religious identity. Therefore, it was necessary to forge actionswhich would carry the message of women equality without underminingtheir religious beliefs. Such global movements as 'Musawah'[2] or 'Equality' (in Arabic) and 'Sisters in Islam'[3]carry the illuminating message of justice and

---

[2] Musawah was spearheaded by twelve women, from countries as diverse as Egypt, Gambia, Turkey and Pakistan, who spent two years laying out the movement's guiding principles. It was officially launched in 2009 at a meeting in Kuala Lumpur that brought together 250 Muslim activists, scholars, legal practitioners and policy-makers from forty-seven nations. The organization is currently based in Malaysia, but will periodically move its secretariat and leadership council from country to country.Elizabeth Segran, *'The Rise Of The Islamic Feminists:Muslim Women are Fighting For Their Rights From Within Islamic Tradition, Rather Than Against It.'*Available atwww.musawah.org/rise-islamic-feminists accessed on 13/09/2015

[3] Musawah's approach is modeled on a Malaysian organization called Sisters in Islam, which works with Islamic scholars to produce workshops and books that explain that Islam does not mandate injustice. Zainah Anwar, one of Musawah's key architects, founded Sisters in Islam in 1988 and has made it an important political and religious force in Malaysia. According to Anwar, many Muslim women spend their entire lives believing that their oppression is justified by Islamic teachings, such as the concept of a husband's authority over his wife. For years, she has gone into rural towns to show women that Islam supports gender equality. "When they are exposed to this new knowledge, they feel duped," says Anwar. "All these years, they believed that their

equality for Muslim women within the Islamic framework. With strong belief in the egalitarian tone of Islam and Islamic principles these transnational movements propagate that gender hierarchies are products of male interpretations in flagrant dereliction of the spirit of Islam. Therefore, the global call to read and interpret Quran in women friendly manner has emerged. Without rejecting their religion and faith, Muslim feminist consciousness seeks greater equality and justice.

What emerged is that Islamic feminism as a discourse of Muslim feminine consciousness that derive its mandate from the Quran and Sunnah not only seeks gender equality and justice but also out rightly rejects the public-private dichotomy.Islamic feminism as a movement "insist on a return to the Quran and employ principles of contextual and rational analysis that disputes traditionally accepted beliefs about women …"[4] Explicating the idea of total rejection of gender discrimination, Islamic feminism calls for implementation of gender equality in both private and public institutions and everyday life.Islamic feminism therefore is not a product or manifestation of Muslim culture but one that engages Islamic theology because at its core it distinctly draws upon canonical principles and traditions. Based on the broader Quranic ideal of equality

---

suffering in the form of abandonment, polygamy and beatings was all in the name of God." *Ibid.*

[4] <u>Rachelle Fawcett</u>, '*The Reality and Future of Islamic feminism: What Constitutes An "Islamic Feminism", And Where Is It Headed?* Available at www.aljazeera.com/indepth/opinion/2013/03/201332715585855781.html accessed on 13/09/2015

of all '*Ummah*' (The whole Muslim community), it seeks Islamic principles and traditions as operative value in both public and private sphere.

Stressing upon 'inclusivity', the proponents of Islamic feminist consciousness (as Amina Wadud and Asma Sayeed) through their intellectual pursuits advocate the rightful claim to personal moral authority.Encountering their culture and traditions in their respective societal settings, the Muslim feminists prioritize the need to create their own course to knowledge and action and move forward addressing their fundamental concerns of justice and equality weeding out traditional dogmas. Reconstructing female authority they cry for freedom from violence seeking personal space of worship and prayer.The Muslim feminists staunchly propagate that discriminatory cultural practices among Muslims is not consistent with Islamic normative teachings.Passing religious knowledge in a matrilineal tradition by means of story-telling, reminiscence ofhistorical figures[5] as remembering simple ahistorical argumentsand rhetoricthe Muslim feminists seek both feminine and religious activism and in the process forge ties on the broader platform of feminist consciousness.

---

[5] At one time in Islamic history it was not uncommon to see learned or saintly Muslim women, and the presence of these women did not necessarily mean that they all agreed on women's roles, just as we don't today, but their existence created a more balanced and accessible theology with a greater degree of accountability. By reclaiming that history, women find their footing and support in Islamic feminine discourse.*Ibid.*

Despite the fact that the ethical tone of Quran is egalitarian and non-discriminatory, the commentators and interpreters of religious texts historically have interpreted them so as to affect male superiority by offering interpretations radically different from the true spirit of traditional scriptures. To the narrow interpretations of Islamic religious principles offered by religious commentators the developments in the Muslim world have also radically contributed in making Muslim women invisible in the public realm.[6]

Perhaps, the greatest task of the movement is to challenge traditionally held beliefs on authority with intelligent and informed dialogue because the aim is not to create a hierarchy with women at the top of the social ladder but to reinforce the egalitarian social structure in which gender is not the defining factor of authority. By remaining open to continued pursuit for truth and justice, the Muslim feminists remain implacably opposed to any social roles being determined bygender.

---

[6] … Since the rise of political Islam in the second part of the century, the battle between tradition and modernity in which Muslim women are still caught must be conducted in a religious language and framework, where jurisprudential constructions of gender can be re-examined and the patriarchal mandates of fiqh can be challenged. The legal gains and losses of women in Iran, and now in Afghanistan and Iraq, testify to the fact that there can be no sustainable gains unless patriarchal notions of family and gender relations are debated, challenged and redressed within an Islamic framework. Ziba Mir-Hosseini (2006), *Muslim Women's Quest for Equality: Between Islam and Feminism*, Critical Enquiry, Vol. 32, No. 4, The University of Chicago Press, p. 644.

SOCIAL JUSTICE AND GENDER EQUALITY IN ISLAM

One important area of campaign for Islamic feminists has been the Sharia principles. The Sharia principles have come under scrutiny and often questions are raised raise, 'Do sharia principles promote gender equality and justice? Is Sharia Stagnant and immune to change? Can they be changed to meet the modern needs of equality and justice? Can Sharia promote feminism and if then how? With a host of such and other related questions in mind, it is pertinent to define sharia at the onset.

It is pertinent here to identify the sources of sharia or what constitutes sharia principles. The rights that are granted to Muslim women owes its origin to '*Quran*', '*Sunnah*' (Traditions of the Prophet), '*Ijma*'[7], '*Qiyas*'[8]

---

[7] Considered as a third source of laws after the Quran and the Sunna, consensus or 'ijma' represented the ultimate sanctioning authority which guaranteed the ultimate infallibility of those positive legal rulings and methodological principles that are universally agreed upon by sunni scholars. Wael B. Hallaq (1997) *A History of Islamic Legal Theories - An Introduction to Sunni Usul al-Fiqh*, U.K: Cambridge University Press, p. 75. Consensus (*ijma*) is commonly taken to mean the unanimous agreement amongst those who are learned in the religion at a particular time on a specific issue, though this is a matter of debate. '*Islam, Land & Property: Research Series. Paper 3: Islamic Law, Land and Methodologies.*'United Nations Human Settlements Programme (UN-HABITAT) 2005, p. 10.

[8] Qiyas is defined as establishing the relevance of a ruling in one case to another case because of a similarity in the attribute, reason or cause upon which the ruling was based. Standish Grove Grandy (1870) *The 'Hedaya' or Guide, A Commentary*

and *'Ijtihad'*[9]As source of Sharia principles the *Quran* and *Sunnah*(Prophetic Traditions) remain divine and immutable whereas the other three as manifestations of human endeavour and interpretations remain amenable to vagaries. Though Sharia principles are often dubbed as unchangeable and stagnant but in reality it is neither

---

on the Mussulman Laws, London: W[M] H. Allen & Company, 2nd ed., p. 566. Qiyas, translated as analogical deduction is the fourth source of Islamic law. As a source of law, it comes into operation in matters which have not been covered by a text of the Quran or tradition (the term tradition is used interchangeably with the Hadith of the Prophet Mohammed), nor determined by consensus of opinion. The law is, thus, deduced from what has been laid down by any of these authorities, by the use of Qiyas.C*ffn,1*, p. 9 (footnotes)

[9] An important source of Sharia, but one which is usually known as a juristic technique in Islamic jurisprudential terms is ijtihad. In the literal sense, the term implies striving hard or strenuousness, but technically it means exercising independent juristic reasoning to provide answers when the Quran and Sunna are silent on a particular subject. Ijtihad was meant to occupy a central place in juristic deduction. A person qualified to carry out ijtihad is known as mujtahid. It is in the doctrine of ijtihad that the Islamic legal doctrine was meant to find its evolutionary path. Historically, however, with the emergence of the four schools of juristic thought, it was declared that 'the doors of ijtihadhad closed forever' and that independent juristic reasoning and hence legal development in keeping with the times, was precluded forever. This position has been challenged by many Muslim scholars who believe that ijtihadis an on-going intellectual pursuit and cannot be discontinued. It is a process of judicial reasoning to interpret or reinterpret rules for new situations arising over time for which the Quran and Sunna have no specific stipulations. *Ibid*, pp. 9-10

static nor fixed. Sharia has an inbuilt mobility as "the term Sharia' means a watering place, a flowing stream, where both animals and humans comes to drink water. Stagnant and standing water is not Sharia.'[10]

As Fazlur Rahman opines Sharia principles is "the totality of Divine Will as revealed through the Prophet, it denotes the highway to good life …", while fiqh denotes "the process of human endeavor to discern and extract legal rules from the sacred sources of Islam: that is, the *Quran* and the *Sunnah*."[11] Thus what emerges is that in contrast to *Quran* and *Sunnah* as eternal and sacred;fiqh is human and temporal.

Towards the end of the 1980's Islamic feminist voices grounding the legitimacy of their movement in Islam gave the clarion call of 'Back to Sharia' and effectively questioned the patriarchal interpretations of the Holy Scriptures by male jurists. Strongly challenging the hegemony of patriarchal interpretations of *Quran* and *Sunnah* (Prophetic Traditions) the feminist voices has exposed that gender insensitivity are male constructionsrather than manifestation of '*Divine Will*'. The foundation of the movement is based on the argument that changes in the lives of Muslim women can be ushered in only by engaging with sacred Islamic texts and Islamic jurisprudence (fiqh). The demand raised was that of re-examining the patriarchal jurisprudential constructions and mandate of 'fiqh'. This

---

[10] *Ibid*, p. 10

[11] Ziba Mir-Hosseini, '*Towards Gender Equality: Muslim Family Laws and the Shari'ah*', Available at www.musawah. orgdocspubswantedWanted-ZMH-EN.pdf accessed on 15/09/2015, p. 25

forced both the religious intellectuals and the ordinary men to rethink the notions of Sharia and Islamic law.

During the late 1980's AbdolkarimSoroush challenged the traditional notions of fiqh and distinguished between religion and religious knowledge. Soroush pointed out that while religion is sacred and immutable religious knowledge is evolutionary in character; it is essentially human construction. The champions of equal rights for Muslim women opposed the traditional and ideological construction of Islamic principles and displaying pragmatic vigour pointed out the flexibility of the human understanding of Islam. Though gender hierarchies and discrimination on the basis of gender is diametrically opposite to Islam, nevertheless such unwarranted practices have sought legitimacy in the name of traditions and customary practices. Therefore, complications and confrontations arise due to the interface between traditional practices and religious injunctions. Based on the twin pillars of equality and non-discrimination the women movement seek real and meaningful equal treatment in overcoming all past and present discriminations.

Muslim women rights activists and feminist scholarship have questioned the patriarchal premises of Islamic texts. For instance, they have questioned the classical principles on marriage and divorce which are claimed to be divinely ordained as put forward by the traditionalists. Islamic feminist scholarship have questioned as to how far the traditionalists interpretation of Islamic texts is in consonance with the principle of ethics and rationality inherent in Islam. They vehemently argue that the motive of male interpreters have been to exclude women from learning and producing religious knowledge so as to monopolize the whole religious domain. With the aim of subduing women's voice the traditional male jurists have rendered social practices and traditions into fixed entities and incorporated them in Islamic jurisprudence.

READING THE QURAN

Recent researches have drawn attention towards the principle of equality between genders in the *Quran*. The *Quran* and *Sunnah* are unequivocal in stating that though men and women differ physicallythey are equal before the *Almighty*. The *Quran* provide certain guidelines when defining human-relationship which inform the thought and behaviour of people in dealing with each other. Apart from the core values of '*taqwa*' (Piety) and '*ihsan*' (doing well) the *Quran* promotes gender equality through the cardinal principles of '*adl*' (justice) and '*musawah*' (equality).

The spirit of equality and just treatment is evident throughout the Quran and encompasses all aspects of private and public life.The egalitarian tone of the *Quran* is evident from the following passages,

> *Chapter 3 Verse 195 (3:195) reads, "Never will I allow to be lost the work of [any] worker among you, whether male or female; you are of one another. So those who emigrated or were evicted from their homes or were harmed ... I will surely remove from them their misdeeds, and I will surely admit them to gardens beneath which rivers flow as reward from Allah ..."*

Chapter 4 Verse 7 (4:7) reads, "There is a share for men and a share for women from what is left by parents and those nearest related, whether the property be small or large - a legal share."

Chapter 4 Verse 32 (4:32)reads, "And wish not for the things in which Allah has made some of you to excel others. For men there is reward for what they have earned, (and likewise) for women there is reward for what they have earned ..."

Chapter 4 Verse 33 (4:33)reads, "And to everyone, We have appointed heirs of that (property) left by parents and relatives. To those also with whom you have made a pledge (brotherhood), give them their due portion (by Wasiyyah - will) ..."

Chapter 4 Verse 124(4:124) reads, "And whoever does righteous deeds, whether male or female ... those will enter Paradise and will not be wronged, [even as much as] the speck on a date seed."

Chapter 4 Verse 135 (4:135) reads, "O you who have believed, be persistently standing firm in justice ... even if it be against yourselves or parents and relatives. Whether one is rich or poor ... So follow not [personal] inclination, lest you not be just ..."

Chapter 5 Verse 8(5:8) "O you who believe! Stand out firmly ... as just witnesses; and let not the enmity and hatred of others make you avoid justice. Be just: that is nearer to piety; …"

Chapter 9 Verse 71 (9:71) reads, "The believing men and believing women are allies of one another. They enjoin what is right and forbid what is wrong …."

Chapter 16 Verse 97(16:97) reads,"Whoever does righteousness, whether male or female, while he is a believer - We will surely cause him to live a good life, and … will surely give them their reward [in the Hereafter] according to the best of what they used to do."

Chapter 35 Verse 35(35:35) reads, "Indeed, the Muslim men and Muslim women, the believing men and believing women … and the men who remember Allah often and the women who do so - for them Allah has prepared forgiveness and a great reward."

Chapter 39 Verse 6 (39:6) reads, "He created you from one soul. Then He made from it its mate …"

Chapter 40 Verse 40(40:40) reads, "Whoso doeth an ill-deed, he will be repaid the like thereof, while whoso doeth right, whether male or female, and is a believer, (all) such will enter the Garden (of Bliss), therein will they have abundance without measure."

Chapter 49 Verse 13(49:13) reads, "O mankind, indeed We have created you from male and female … Indeed, the most noble of you in the sight of Allah is the most righteous of you. Indeed, Allah is Knowing and Acquainted."

Chapter 57 Verse 12(57:12) reads, "On the Day you see the believing men and believing women, their light proceeding before them and on their right, [it will be said], "Your good tidings today are [of] gardens beneath which rivers flow, wherein you will abide eternally." That is what the great attainment is."

CONCLUSION

In the *Hadith*[12] the *Prophet* is said to espouse the cause of complete equality. In his last address to the Muslims on the occasion of '*The Last Pilgrimage*' (*HijjatulWida*) the *Prophet* said, "All people are equal, as equal as the teeth of a comb. There is no claim of merit of an Arab over a non-Arab or of a white over a black person: Only God-fearing people merit a preference with God. Thus men and women are equal."[13]

The equality of both genders is signified from the fact that "…God has made us from the same soul', (Quran 39:6) and on the basis of this fundamental truth any discrimination and attempt to subordinate women or project them as vulnerable is only artificial and man-made.Islam envisions the role of both male and female as complementary and not as competing. Any customs or social practices decrying women as inferior to men stand in direct opposition to the letter and spirit of *Quran*. The *Quran* repeatedly calls for equal treatment of women (Quran 2:228, 231) and reprimands thosetreating females as inferior and males as superior.

We often notice gross negligence of *Quranic injunctions* and *Prophetic Traditions* of equality and justiceboth in public and personal lives of Muslim women. Without

---

[12] Generally pronounced in Urdu as '*Hadis*' and used in India as equivalent to '*Sunnah*', this word denotes Traditions of the Prophet collected by his companions and their disciples. Tahir Mahmood (1976), *An Indian Civil Code and Islamic Law,* Bombay, N. M. Tripathi, p. 65 (footnotes)

[13] Cf*fn 1*, p. 18.

falling into the mistake of calling for revision or rethinking of *Quranic injunctions*what needs to be rectified are the fallible human interpretations and practices. The diverse discriminatory practices practised against women as vulnerable sex is often due to different cultural influences. Therefore, the current situation warrants implementing the *Quranic Principles* in its true spirit which alone has the potential of overcoming the dichotomy of gender-politics. The dual combination of feminine consciousness with correct knowledge of equity and justice principles bears the potential of mitigating gender inequalities and empowering the 'so called' vulnerable sex.

REFERENCES

The Quran

Elizabeth Segran, *'The Rise Of The Islamic Feminists: Muslim Women are Fighting For Their Rights From Within Islamic Tradition, Rather Than Against It,'* Available atwww.musawah.org/rise-islamic-feminists accessed on 13/09/2015

"*Islam, Land & Property: Research Series. Paper 3: Islamic Law, Land and Methodologies.*" United Nations Human Settlements Programme (UN-HABITAT) 2005, p. 10.

ShaheenSardar Ali (ed. 2006), *'Conceptualising Islamic Law, CEDAW and Women's Human Rights in Plural Legal Settings: A Comparative Analysis of Application of CEDAW in Bangladesh, India and Pakistan*, available at www.unifem.org.in.PDFcomplete%20study.pdf.pdf

Rachelle Fawcett, *'The Reality and Future of Islamic feminism: What Constitutes An "Islamic Feminism", And Where Is It Headed?* Available at www.aljazeera.com/indepth/opinion/2013/03/201332715585855781.html accessed on 13/09/2015

Standish Grove Grandy (2nd ed., 1870) *The 'Hedaya' or Guide, A Commentary on the Mussulman Laws*, London: W^M H. Allen & Company,

Tahir Mahmood (1976), *An Indian Civil Code and Islamic Law,* Bombay, N. M. Tripathi, p. 65 (footnotes)

Wael B. Hallaq (1997) *A History of Islamic Legal Theories - An Introduction to Sunni Usul al-Fiqh*, U.K: Cambridge University Press,

Ziba Mir-Hosseini (2006), *Muslim Women's Quest for Equality: Between Islam and Feminism*, Critical

Enquiry, Vol. 32, No. 4, The University of Chicago Press pp.629-645

Ziba Mir-Hosseini, "Towards Gender Equality: Muslim Family Laws and the Shari'ah", Available at www. musawah.orgdocspubswantedWanted-ZMH-EN.pdf accessed on 15/09/2015

Chapter 11

Khaled Hosseini's 'A Thousand Splendid Suns'- a Story of Motherhood and Sustenance

DR. LILY MONDAL,
Assistant Professor
Govt. Training College, Hooghly

Khaled Hosseini's 'A Thousand Splendid Suns' graphically portrays the plight of women in the face of horror and bloodshed. It tells the story of two women -Mariam and Laila whose lives become desperate struggle in the hands of cruelty and brutality. Their endurance to sustain lives is heart-wrenching and leaves one gasping for breath. Vivid picturisation of troubled country and the plight of women caught in the whirlpool of tyranny make Hosseni's work stunning and splendid. What is to be noted that how women can bond beyond imagination and how they can sustain the lives of their children - are the central themes of the novel. The symbol of 'Matryoshka dolls' runs through the novel. Like the 'Matryoshka dolls' which have similar smaller dolls inside them, in this story Mariam holds Laila and Aziza, whom Laila bore in her womb.

The novel is about two women Mariam and Laila in particular and involves other women in general. Both Mariam and Laila happen to marry the same person

Rasheed, a hard-hearted, thoroughly cruel man. Mariam is the illegitimate daughter of Jalil and Nana, housekeeper in Jalil's house. Nana is cast out and is forced to live in 'kolba' outside Herat; there in the 'kolba' Mariam was born. Jalil was one of the wealthiest men in Herat who owned a cinema and had good connections. He had three wives and nine legitimate children. As Mariam was born out of marriage and Nana was an uneducated maid, they did not get a place in Jalil's mansion. Instead they were forced to live in a 'kolba', where Mariam spends the first fifteen years of her life. Jalil used to visit Mariam on Thursdays with lots of gifts, stories and information about the outside world. So Jalil was like a fresh shower in Mariam's life with whom she never felt to be unwanted though Nana had already mentioned to her that she was a 'harami'- a bastard who would never get acceptance in Jalil's life. She had warned Mariam:

> "Learn this now and learn it well,
> my daughter: Like a compass needle that
> points north, a man's accusing finger
> always finds a woman. Always You
> remember that, Mariam."(7)

Nana had sufficient reason to say this as Jalil had said to his wives that she had forced herself on him. That it was Nana's fault. Nana had rued: "this is what it means to be a woman in this world" (6)

What it means to be a woman in this world is portrayed through the lives of four generation of women- Nana-her daughter Mariam- Laila, almost like Mariam's daughter- Aziza, daughter of Laila.

Mariam is made to join Jalil's family after Nana's suicide. She was shattered but yet hopeful about her stay with Jalil, her father. There she encounters all the humiliation and finally is married off to a man who was almost thirty years older than her. Mariam had pinned all her hopes in Jalil for whom she wished100 years of life. But the same man got rid of her. Mariam's grief is unfathomable and she declares to her father:

> "Don't come, I won't see you. Don't you come. I don't want to hear from you. Ever. Ever."(50)

Mariam travels six-hundred-and- fifty-kilometer bus trip to reach Deh-Mazang, the place of Rasheed who believes that "…a woman's face is her husband's business only."(63)

However, Mariam accepts her fate and hopes that 'they would make good companions after all' (77). Mariam becomes pregnant and was very happy about her pregnancy. But unfortunately Mariam loses this child. For Rasheed too it was unbearable loss. Mariam swallowed the pain remembering her mother Nana's words: "How quietly we endure all that falls upon us"(82). Mariam was washed over by the grief and was tossed upside down. She missed the baby in a crippling manner, a being whom she had never seen. Mariam grieved for the baby who had made her happy for a while. She accused herself for the loss:

> "She became furious with herself for sleeping in the wrong position, for eating meals thatwere too spicy, for eating not

enough fruit, for drinking too much tea"(84)

Mariam even accused God for not granting the happiness WHICH He had granted to many other women. Butthen she thought that it was sacrilege to think like this for Allah can not be spiteful. For Mullah Faizullah had whispered in her head:

> "Blessed is He in Whose hand is the kingdom, and He Who has power over all things. Who created death and life thay He may try you."(85)

Mariam wants a proper burial for the child and does so finally by digging a hole and putting the suede coat brought by Rasheed for the baby and shoveling dirt over it. She squatted by the mound and closed her eyes praying:

> "Give sustenance, Allah
> Give sustenance to me."(87)

In the next four years of marriage Mariam learns how much a woman could tolerate when she was afraid. She had to endure Rasheed's shifting moods, volatile temperament, his kicks, slaps, punches. In the four years Mariam had had six more cycles of hopes raised and then dashed to the ground:

> "…each loss, each collapse, each trip to the doctor more crushing for Mariam than the last" (89)

And with each disappointment Rasheed drew apart from her more and became more resentful. Mariam tried every possible way to soothe him but nothing she did pleased him. She submitted to his wants and demands yet he found fault with her. She had failed him seven times to return a son which made her a burden to him.

Part Two of the story starts with another woman's story Laila, deeply in love with Tariq, her childhood sweetheart. Laila's father, a university educated man wanted Laila to be educated in life:

> "Marriage can wait, education cannot. You're a very, very bright girl. Truly, you are. Youcan be anything you want, Laila. I know this about you. And I also know that when the war is over, Afganistan is going to need you as much as its men, may be even more. Because a society has no chance of success if its women are uneducated, Laila. No chance."(103)

Laila always 'felt excluded when the talk turned to her brothers' (108). Laila grew up at the backdrop of Soviet invasion of Afganistan. Laila's brothers went to the warfront leaving Laila's mother forlorn and dissatisfied. Her brothers die in the battlefield leaving Laila's mother bereaved forever and never bereft of ailments. At the morning Rasheed's wife Mariam also comes. But then both Laila and Mariam were unaware of their future fate and bonding.

In April1998, Babi brings home the news that Geneva that the Soviets have signed the treaty to leave Afganistan within nine months. Afganistan would be free. Laila and Tariq grew older and Laila's mother is worried about their relationship. "It's about you and Tariq. He's a boy, you see, and, as such, what does he care about reputation? But you? The reputation of a girl."(146) But Laila had a point that if her father had asked about Tariq it was alright. But her mother has neglected her all these years and suddenly enquiring about her. Yet Laila and Tariq spent time together. In the streets Tariq was Laila's lifeline in the streets. The treacherous shifting boundaries within Kabul created many warlords. Everywhere there were killing and looting but "it was a harmless thing to sit here beneath a tree and kiss Tariq." (159)

Ultimately Laila and Tariq make love and Tariq wants to marry her. Tariq is also scheduled to leave Afganistan as the unrest grew day by day. But Laila can not accompany Tariq for she can't leave her father. But ultimately Laila's parents also decide to move. But before they could make it out everything was crushed and Laila Was left in living in death.

Part Three of the Novel opens with Mariam tending Laila. In the following chapter an unknown man called Abdul Sarif comes with the news of Tariq's death. Laila's love is dead. She is left alone in this world. Mariam sensed that Rasheed's kindness is somewhat fishy. Ultimately her worse fear comes true. Rasheed's proposes to marry Laila to legitimize the relationship. Raheed reasons out that he is a downright charitable man who is providing Laila a sanctuary and a husband. Mariam is dumbstruck and yet Mariam pleads. "Eighteen years," Mariam said. "And I never asked you for a thing. Not one thing. I'm asking now."(192) But Rasheed finalises by saying by saying "The way I see it, I deserve a medal."(193) At this point Mariam is thirty three, Laila fourteen and Rasheed above sixty. Mariam told Laila at night that Rasheed wants the answer by that morning. Laila surprised Mariam by saying "He can have it now," "My answer is yes". (193)

Though Laila had decided to leave for Pakistan and even after Abdul Sharif's visit's she had wished to escape but amidst all the uncertaitiess she becomes aware that she had missed a cycle:

> 'A part of Tariq still alive inside her, sprouting tiny arms, growing transluscent hands. How could she jeopardize the only thing she had left of him, of her old life?' (196)

She knew she did 'spectacularly unfair to Mariam'. Her decision was tough but 'Laila already saw the sacrifices a mother had to make. Virtue was only the first'(196) the marriage took place and Laila tried to leave the impression that prior to the marriage she was a virgin.

Rasheed did not spare a chance to humiliate Mariam by calling her 'harami'- a bastard: 'Have you told her, Mariam, have you told her that you are a 'harami'?' (199) But Laila wants to heal the wounds of Mariam who was greatly hurt by the word 'harami' even at the age of thirty three. Laila approaches to apologise earnestly for what Rasheed said in front of her. Mariam expressed her desire to talk to her and finally they talk. 'Laila looked relieved' (201)

Rasheed cares for Laila too much as she is pregnant and Rasheed expects it to be a boy: "It's going to be a big boy. My son will be a pahalwan! Like his father."(209) In the spring of 1993, Laila delivers her daughter. Rasheed could not accept that it is not a boy. He does not even buy the newborn clothes and Laila had to make her wear all boys' dress already bought by Rasheed. Very soon Rasheed wants to make love to get a boy. But Laila's denial is crushing him. Finally Rasheed opts his own cruel way to heat Mariam with his leather belt as if Mariam taught Laila to deny him sex. Laila runs to Mariam's rescue and finally surrenders to Rasheed'd wish. That night Mariam was awakened thrice from her sleep. The rumble of rockets, the cry of the baby and finally thirst pulled her out of bed. That night Mariam went to the baby, lifted her in her arms and sat there until the baby started snoring. Mariam's motherly pleasure is satisfied as if she is mother of both Laila and Aziza, Laila's daughter.

Two days' later, Laila get a stack of baby clothes, neatly folded- they were all made by Mariam who had no use of them. That night Laila comes down to thank Mariam for the dresses. Mariam also acknowledges that 'the other night, when he..Nobody's ever stood up for me before.'(223) Mariam and Laila exchanges words and Mariam warns that "And you gave him a daughter. So you see, your sin is even less forgivable than mine." (223) They talk over 'chai and halwa'. That night they start bonding. "Laila knew that they were not enemies any longer"(224) From that night on they finished their chores together.

Gradually one day Mariam let go from her mouth like blood gushing from an artery. She said everything about her past life, about her father Jalil and his wives and about his mother's suicide. Laila too unfolds herself. Mariam was surprised that over the last months 'Laila and Aziza – harami like herself, as it turned out, had become extensions of her, and now, without them, the life Mariam had tolerated for so long suddenly seemed intolerable'. (229) Laila told Mariam: 'We're leaving this spring, Aziza and I, come with us Mariam'(229) Suddenly it seemed to Mariam that two new flowers have sprouted in her life.

Next year (1994) one spring morning the three of them leave in a taxi for the bus stop. Unfortunately there the man Wakil cheated them in the name of buying tickets for them. They end up in a police station in Trabaz Kan Intersection. Finally they are driven back home to face Rasheed's vengeance. He locks both of them, without food and water even for the child. He alsoannounces if she does like this in future he would make Laila watch what he does to Mariam first and then to Aziza and lastly to Laila.

In 1996 Taliban regime came and Rasheed seemed to be excited as he said "I, for one, will shower them with rose petals"(245) Talibans declared rules to be followed which infuriated Laila: "They can't make half of the population stay home and do nothing,"(249) But Rasheed who had tortured Mariam and Laila agreed with the Talibans. The same year Laila becomes pregnant and wonders if she could love Rasheed's child. But finally she resolves that her war was against Rasheed. 'The baby was blameless. And there had been enough killing already.'(253) In September 1997 Laila delivers Rasheed's boy Jalmai, the name Rasheed had thought years before when Mariam was pregnant.

As days passed, Rasheed was forced to drop his work at shoe shop. He tried work from one place to another. They were amid dire poverty which prompted Rasheed to propose to Laila to admit Aziza to an orphanage and finally in April 2001 Aziza is shifted to Kaeth-She orphanage. Laila was heartbroken. Laila often visited the orphanage along with Rasheed and Mariam. Rasheed waited outside and they went in to meet Aziza but gradually Rasheed relented to accompany them. When Laila tried alone she was often beaten up by the Talibans –whipped, whacked, knocked and sent back home. Laila wondered: '…that a human body could withstand this much beating, this viciously, this regularly, and keep functioning.'(287)

And in between all these uncertainties Tariq returns astounding Laila. Jalmai resented Tariq's presence and did not like him. Moreover he informs Rasheed: 'MAMMY HAS A new friend' (297) When Rasheed comes to know that he has visited, he burst out in anger. Laila accused him of duping her and lying to her. In return Rasheed roared: "You think I didn't figure it out? About your harami? You take me for a fool, you whore?"(300) During Tariq's visit Laila unfurls everything. How she was lied, why she was forced to marry Rasheed: "Because there was a bigger reason why I married him. Ther's something. You don't know, Tariq. Some one. I tell you." (303) On Tariq's side there is no accusation, no blame. He finds what Rasheed had done to her. He wants to take her with him: "I know you're a married woman and a mother now."(305)

When Rasheed comes to know about Tariq's frequent visits he becomes infuriated and locks Jalmai and thrashes Laila on the ground and is on the verge of killing Laila. Mariam on the spur of the moment in a move to save Laila hits Rasheed to death with a shovel. Laila and Mariam hide the dead body in the tool shed. They think of their future course of life. They plan to leave the country and find a place to live in peace. But when the time comes Mariam asks Laila to leave with the children and to think like a mother: "Think like a mother. I am" (319) Mariam is grief-stricken for Jalmai as he has lost his dear father: "I'll never escape your son's grief. How do I look at him? How do I bring myself to look at him, Laila jo?" Mariam wants Laila to start a new life. As for her:

> "…for me, it ends here. There's nothing more I want. Everything I'd ever wished for as a little girl you've already given me. You and your children have made me so very happy. It's all right, Laila jo. This is all right. Don't be sad." (319)

And Mariam ends up in the prison where she gets life sentence.

Part Four of the novel is all about Tariq and Laila's life in Pakistan. And when Laila returns to Kabul she starts working with Jaman, the orphanage director. While taking the class there Laila feels the movement in the belly. Though naming game at home figures all the male names if it is a girl Laila has already named her.

With this the symbol of 'Matryoshka dolls' comes full circle. Laila is carrying Mariam in her womb. When Laila and Mariam were sitting together and thinking of their future life somewhere remote and safe, Mariam says: "Somewhere with trees," she said. Yes. Lots of trees."(315) as Mariam wants to be in the lap of Mother Nature – to be cherished and loved. Nature has the all encompassing power which can alleviate all the pain of women, who bear children and keep the wheel on moving. Such is the power of motherhood; such is the greatness of mothers who sustain the lives of their children scarifying even their virtue. The novel not only depicts the saga of motherhood through generations but it is also an eye-opener towards the gross violence, torture, humiliation and discrimination against women beyond borders. At the same time it shows the basic instinct of mothers to bear and protect children in any crushing situation.

BIBLIOGRAPHY

1. Hosseini, Khaled: A Thousand Splendid Suns, London, Bloomsbury, 2007.

Chapter 12

BEING *SITA*: Being Cursed; How Popular Narrative Constructs the Perceptions of 'Being Ideal'

ANUSUYA ROY
Senior Research Fellow
Department of Sociology
University of Jadavpur

The broadcast of Rama*yana* in Doordarshan from 1986-1988 brought about a new consciousness amongst the people in India. It is not only the telecast of the serial that Indian Hindus were bothered about, but rather, they considered it to be sacred. As according to Richman's study, some responded to the imagery of Rama played by Arun Govil and Sita by Deepsha Chikaliaa was similar to icons of Rama enshrined in the temples. Hence, before watching they used to bathe, and garland the shrines as they considered it to be a religious experience. The text of Rama*yana* has helped to bring about common sense conceptions of Indian culture, community, and identity (Purnima Mankekar). In response to this viewership Lutgendorf(1989) commented that it is for the very first time in the history of Indian viewership, the whole population was gathered and concentrated on the same event with the similar enthusiasm. On the other hand,

Thapar is of the view that, the telecast of Rama*yana*, did not concern to the vast majority of Indians, but rather to the specific group of people, mainly the middle class or the aspirants to the same status. She establishes the stance of the state who acts like the patron of art, and favors a social group that has a much-yielded influence on the society; and hence the middle class. It was during this time when the state was restructuring and rearticulating itself into turning of Indian nation to that of Hindu nation (Purnima Mankekar). The state tends to enhance the idea of national culture, which is brought about through Rama*yana*. It is also that Rama*yana* does not belong to any specific moment of history; it is still present in the day to day lives of Hindus.

There are varieties and versions of Rama*yana*-s told and retold, which narrates the location and ideology of those who appropriates it. Rama*yana*, which have been narrated to us throughout our childhood, had been a fusion of many versions. Thapar in this context has cleared the concerns that "*the appropriation of the story by multiplicity of groups means the multiplicity of versions, through which the social aspirations and ideological concerns are articulated. The story in these versions included significant variations, which changed the conceptualization of characters, event, and meaning.*" Hence, there lies the homogenization of narrative which results into the cultural loss. Pedantically, the Valimiki's *Ramayana* was written in Sanskrit, and later rewritten by Tulsidas in the language, which is accessible to the non- literate (non-Brahmin) population of India during the 16th century.

In my quest to understand the nature and development of ideologies promoted in Rama*yana*, as a part of our day to day discourse, I tried to gather the resources from an authoritative source of Valmiki *Ramayana* and *Ramacharitamanas* by Tulsidas translated by Gita Press (Gorakhpur edition). In every Indian regional language, it emerged as an eminent poem, and with regular recitation and annual religious productions. Khan comments that it is one the text which could be considered as a manual of Hindu ethics. The *Ramayana* has carried the traditional Hindu ideologies to the youngest and simplest of many generations. It is worth noting that though Valmiki created Rama, yet Indians got to have the real taste of the character through Swami Tulsidas's *Ramcharitamanas* in the 16th century. The original Rama*yana* was a Sanskrit text, while as Tulsidas wrote in Awadhi, which was more of a courtly dialect. The latter text glorified the existence of the prince of Ayodhya, who could be termed as the paragon of virtues, which includes trustworthiness, loyalty, courteous, helpful, kind, obedient, brave and reverent. Philip Lutgendorf rightly commented that Rama is the Eagle Scout of Hindu mythology, which implies that he possessed those qualities which are lacking in Krishna (from *the Mahabharata*). F.S Growse (1979) furthered that Rama*yana* is more accepted in the Indian Hindu society because of its nature, more appropriately *"absolute avoidance of the slightest approach to any prurience of idea"*. That implies that in a Victorian way of saying that the text lacked sex. Hence, Lutgendorf commented that Indian Hindus had internalized the "sensuality" and "effeminacy" of devotional Hinduism. By extension to this, Rama is considered as *Maryada Purushottam* (ideal/nobleman); the exemplar of social propriety throughout many centuries. Unlike *Mahabharata*, Rama*yana* is made up of a simple and single plot which comprises of love, exploits, and suffering of Prince Rama and Princess Sita. In *Ramcharitamanas*, Tulsidas divinized Rama after Bhakti revival during the 16th century. But in Valmiki Rama*yana*, the moral norms are more established which goes back as far as the *Laws of Manu* which is followed by *Upanishads*. Since Valmiki's creation Sita is still enshrined in the hearts of Hindus along with Janardana, i.e. Krishna. It implies that persons who recite their names secure merit. Alternately, it implies to whom devotees pray for worldly success and liberation.

Though the *Laws of Manu* dictates the gender roles, the mandate for Hindu woman's behavior is hugely drawn from the familiar text like Rama*yana*. Sita is held as the ideal woman throughout many centuries in Indian society. Sita is seen as a shadow of Rama, the ideal man *Marjada Purushumtum*. She is perceived as a woman, who is an epitome of an ideal wife/ companion/ consort and follow the footstep of her husband throughout every thick and thin. Hindus as a mass, maintain the fact that they are well versed with the text of Rama*yana*, but fail to realize that their knowledge of the text lies is the fusion of many versions of the text narrated by various authors. The people have a myopic understanding of Sita who they think that her duty or dharma rests on the fulfillment of her husband's desires. This is well promoted in the text (irrespective of its different versions), that soon after she learns about Rama's resolution to retire to the forest for the span of fourteen years, she also resolves to accompany him. Despite Rama's insistence to abide by her duties as a daughter-in-law, she stands on her judgment. She considers that her dharma will be restored if she remains close to her husband under any circumstances.

Sita also claims that her salvation lies through her ability to serve her husband. In reference to this episode, it would be useful to cite the survey of Mary McGee (1991), who said that while interviewing the Hindu women, she found that it is more important for them to abide by the duties of a marital nexus than to the religious duties which would directly lead to salvation. Mary McGee also commented that through her study, she learnt that according to the interviewees the salvation of a Hindu married woman is tied to her duties to serve her husband, rather than a need of a good husband, healthy child or happy marriage. Spiritual salvation is only achieved by maintaining marital felicity.

Hindu culture is inherently patriarchal and androcentric. This attitude lies in direct conflict with the goddess worship, which holds a significant place in Hinduism. There is the presence of different goddesses who can provide different models of womanhood in subtle ways. I would like to add that women cannot be considered as a homogenous grouping in India, as there is caste, region, class and demographic factors which have an impact on their experiences. In the first instance it might be apparent that *Laws of Manu* is essentially a patriarchal text, yet it also specifies that though women are subservient, they should be revered, and if not, all other rituals will eventually turn into fruitless pursuits. So adhering to Rama*yana* and *Laws of Manu* is also questionable as it provides pan normative ideals, but lacks the specificity, as Hinduism is diversified based on caste, gender and topography.

As commented by Phyllis K Herman, there lies a serious discussion on the grounds that how 'feminine' and 'feminism' are categorized by Hindu woman today.

Has there been a potential relation between the two? The current subordinate position of women in India in terms of social, cultural and religious realm is supported by religious scriptures which form the spine of Hindu traditions. Gender construction in India has its roots stuck in Sita's Agnipariksha, Draupadi Chirharan and Damayanti's compliance with pativrata code. It is not how women have been portrayed in these events, but how it has been projected through expressions of masculinities and patriarchal roles. That is, how the Hindu hegemonic masculinity has used the characters to gain control over women's sexuality. The characters like Sita, Draupadi and Damayanti was created to extract the obedience through the functioning of patriarchy. Women in Modern India fail to acknowledge that 'being Sita' can also imply that in the future, it might lead to death, either by choice or by chance. And the classic examples which suit the main paradigm of *pativrata* are "Sati" and "Sita". The great Hindu narratives provide examples of strong women, who not only took care of themselves, but their husband and families, while experiencing stress and dejections, resisted parental authority but at times reprimanded their husbands.

Herman claims that the models like Rama and Shiva have been activated, in order to serve the masculinity prototype required for Indian nationalism, similarly Kali and Durga also served as models of femininity for certain Hindu states. If the sacrifices of Sita and Sati are considered as most preferable ideals to be emulated by Hindu women, then does it not count that their strengths should retain the ideal for these masses of population? In response to this it can be pointed that both of them have shrines in Ayodhya and Citrakut respectively, which could also imply that both have grounding in Indian feminism, where they are both enshrined and revered like the other male gods in the Hindu religion. The existence of Hindu feminism can be defended on the grounds that the cultural narratives along with the sacred geography gave rise to religious iconography which speaks for Hindu feminism. It won't be wrong to comment that as Sita enters the earth, and *Sati's* body parts are disintegrated and fell on different parts of India, hence the idea of fertility is established and it is unified through the existence of these myths. The Sakti Pithas marked in different parts of India, tends to encompass another story of how the *Puranas* has dealt with the end of Sati. In one version it narrates that Sati's body gets dismembered as *Shiva* proceeds with her corpse, while in the other version there are instances that Vishnu himself hastens the process by gradually cutting the Sati's body and dispersing it. The question is still unanswered as to how the narratives are used to justify the circumstances, according to the conveniences of the mass which at times tries to project masculinities and on the other hand the ideals of femininity?

Rita Sherma questions the idea of divine feminine, which is the combination of female agency and authority. In response to which I would like to forward D.C Sircar (1937) comments about the trails which traces the mythological birth of Sati. Sircar forwarded that it was amongst many others Kalidasa was also one who introduced the story of *Sati* from the *Puranas* to non Brahmin population of India. The great dramatist Kalidasa contemplates the story of *Sati,* who was the daughter of Daksa and wife of Shiva. With certain turn of events she resorts to committing suicide, when her husband was refused to enter the sacrifice her father arranged. *Sati* dies in her sprite to save her husband's honor, similar to Sita, who in order to safeguard her honor and maintain her husband's authority, enters the fire to prove her chastity.

It is strange to note that in Hinduism like any other world religion, the chastity of woman lies in her body. The ultimate salvation lies not only in the feet of her husband, but also her body is owned by him. The spiritual purity lies in the ladder much lower that physical chastity. A popular example can be drawn from the Rama*yana*, in reference to the episode of Ahalya. She is the wife of great sage Gautama, was involved in one amorous activity with Lord Indra. There are different versions in justification of her stance with her knowing that Indra, who took the disguise of her husband, and enticed her into erotic intercourse. The text suggests the later occurrence of this event, though Indra was also cursed by great sage, yet it was much less than her being turned into a stone and was later received liberation through Rama. Is it wrong to suggest that, not only the chastity of a woman is knitted with her husband, but also that she receives salvation only through the hands of another man? The *Laws of Manu* suggests that women have no independent existence apart from men, and the dharma of her lies in the well being of her husband.

Ramayana is seen as a text, which seems to be laden with ideal behavior. The characters of Dasaratha, Rama, Sita, Lakshmana are the exemplars, who seems to illustrate the proper conduct of a father, son, wife and brother respectively. As Ramanujan comments that *"India never changes under the veneers of modern, India still thinks like Vedas"*. That is to say that though the society has changed, Hinduism has also undergone many changes, yet Valmiki's

Ramayana remained the same. Hindu women often recite hymns on *Pancha Mahasatis* or *Pancha Kanya*, who belong to the Hindu pantheon of gods and goddesses. They are mainly Ahalya, Draupadi, Sita, Tara and Mandadoori. If chastity had been the abiding nature to control women's sexuality, how come none of the *"Pancha Satis"(five chaste ladies)* could not actually fulfill the criteria of ideal womanhood? Among the five Satis, four are from *Ramayana*, and one from *Mahabharata*. Ahalya was a woman of exquisite beauty, that she aroused the lust of Indra, who took the form of her husband and enjoyed her. Valmiki commented that Ahalya was well aware of Indra's presence, yet could not resist herself and refuse Indra. In the Hindu way of life, the wife's failure as a *pativrata* lies in the death of her husband before her. Ahalya was left behind to suffer pains and drudgery, when already Gautama, had ascended to the heaven. She can only be liberated by Rama, who, though an avatar of *Vishnu*, yet a distant man and not the husband of Ahalya. How can she be included as one of the five Virgins of *Hindu Nama*? Draupadi had five husbands and failed in fulfilling the arrangement of marriage, which is prescribed in *Dharmasastras*. Sita, though the wife of Rama yet was abducted by Ravana, hence her chastity is also in doubt. Mandadoori, the wife of Ravana, was taken over by Vibishana after the former's death. *Tara* was the wife of Valin but was taken over by Sugriva, and moreover was a drinker. It seems like her situation was similar to that of Mandadoori. So how the ideal those who are in the epics do not fulfill the parameters for which they are celebrated. If considered on the grounds of *dharma*, then it could be stated that amongst the many less heard *Pativratas*, who tends to sacrifice herself for her husband then which strikes up in this aspect is Gandhari. Though forced into marriage, she maintained her dignity by blindfolding herself, as her husband (Dhritarashtra) who was too was deprived of eyesight. The question here lies, that is it the only victorious heroes of the epics are celebrated and not the others despite their sacrifices?

It can be rightfully said that the most controversial of the problems in Rama*yana* had been the trial by fire for Sita. Arvind Kumar on July 1957 published a poem by the name: *Ram Ka Antaradvandana*. That is to say Rama*'s inner conflict*. It mainly focuses on Rama's ambiguous attitude towards Sita once she was rescued from Ravana's prison. The poem dealt with Rama's inner questions with respect to Sita's abduction by Ravana. The poem dealt with certain intrinsic pains which might have occurred to Rama. Firstly, was Sita eloped with Ravana, or she was taken by force. Secondly, did she preserve her chastity while under his power? Finally, if she had been abducted forcefully, whether she in later times, fell in love with Ravana, and does she harbors the same feeling towards him after she returned to Ayodh*ya*. It won't be surprising to note that soon after the publishing of the poem from magazine Sarita, it came under the direct attention of the religious press of Delhi, who were motivated by Arya Samaj, the Sanantan Dharma Sabha, and the Hindu Maha Sabha. Delhi government in following few days banned the magazine, as there was a huge mob protesting while burning an effigy of Arvind Kumar and threats him with lynching. So it becomes quite clear how the episode of trial by fire has been restored in the mind of Hindus throughout the centuries in the hope that how women can be controlled if she trespasses the line of control (*Lakshman Rekha*). This is an important example to mention because it justifies Thapar's comment about how the modern state controls the mass. The subjects have belief in the events in the epics without questioning and hence state also justifies their stance by not rectifying them, but rather supporting them.

It won't be wrong to comment that, Sita when carried away by Ravana, also thought of the world would react to this event. As she herself forced Lakhsmana to follow the trails of Rama, so was there might be some devious scheme which was attached to her motives. It would be worth noticing that how Sita managed to save her chastity while in the captivity for so long. It is similar to the *Helen of Troy*, where the latter rescues the former from *Menelaus*. In the *Bhagavatpurana* or *Ramopakhyana* there was no mention of the ordeal undertaken by Sita. It was a later addition, to justify her chastity. There is also a mention in Valmikian Rama*yana*, where Ravana rapes Rambha the lover of Nalakubera. The latter curses Ravana, by saying that if he ever touches other woman without her consent, then his head will burst into seven pieces. There are various additions later in the Rama*yana*, which not only claims that Sita was untouched, but I can easily draw the hidden inference that Sita's chastity was important to glorify Rama.

The importance of the *Ramayana* for Hindu Indian culture is highly endorsed by Sita's career. G.S Ghurye in *Legacy of* Rama*yana* (1979), commented that the episode of Rama and Sita interacting for the very first time in their private sphere was when Rama announced that he have to retire to the forest for an exile of fourteen years. As from the very beginning of the epic it has been announced that Rama is an obedient son of his father, hence it was his duty to abide by the promise of Dasaratha to his chief queen Kaikeyi (Rama's stepmother). In this very tete-a-tete (Ibid) a cultured Hindu woman actually had shown the doctrine of equality of the sexes. As a dutiful wife, who was also termed as *Pativrata,* Sita showed her resistance to Rama's command which entailed that she would stay back and serve her duties as the daughter-in-law. She responded to Rama's insistence with a pure rational argument which encompassed that 'a mother, sire and son receive lots through their merits. The brother and daughter find their position in terms of their deeds, but it is only a wife who has to share her husband's fate'. Sita was not a docile bearer of the destiny of Rama*yana*, but also at the very same time she questions the decisions of Rama while they were for the very first time in a private closure. Hence, she reprimanded her husband and asserted that if Rama has to retire to the wilds of Dandaka forest, she would surely accompany him. She even used the scriptures to corroborate her stance and cited the example of Savitri who accompanied Satyavan and won him back from the doors of heaven and from the hands of Yama (the god of death). In their journey throughout the Dandaka forest, Rama and Sita came across Atri the mendicant and his wife Anasuya. Valmiki has himself made Atri praise the uniqueness of his wife and considered her as *pativrata*, (dutiful wife of antiquity). The myth says that Anasuya also displayed her presence of mind by ordering the morning to never dawn. In response to Anasuya's praises and compliments, Sita stated inter alia. She answers Anasuya by saying that it is not the duty, to abide to the commands of her husband, but it is also essential on her part to work shoulder to shoulder with him and it should be the basic philosophy of an ideal wife. Here she also tries to place her argument with the example of Savitri and establishes that why it is natural for Hindu women to pay respect and reverence to this lady and observe fast on the full moon day in Jyeshta (June-July) mash (month) to felicitate her for bringing back her husband from the jaws of death.

Smith commented that more the *Ramayana* have evolved throughout the ages, more fantastic and unrealistic it became. It is not only the women in the epics have failed as the ideal model, but there are equal fallacies to be observed in the male characters of the epic. Valmiki in *Kishkinda Kanda*, comments that no sooner Sita was abducted by Ravana, Rama sought the help of Sugriva who was also in distress and struck a deal that if he helped him to rescue Sita, Rama then would assist him to retrieve his kingdom from his brother Valin. Though the pact makes a political sound, yet it must be remembered that Rama instructed Sugriva to invite *Valin* into a combat, and when the two brothers were fighting Rama actually shoots Valin, from a position which told that he was hidden behind the trees. It is quite apparent that Rama failed to abide by the norms of being a Kshatriya, yet he is considered as the ideal king throughout many centuries. This is not only exclusive to Rama*yana* but also in *the Mahabharata*, where Yuddhisthira in collaboration with Krishna fell into the trap and tells a white lie which brings in the formidable death of Drona. This example was essential to cite as Yuddhisthira is also considered as the person who all throughout his life adhered to the norms of *Dharma*. But in the field of Kurukshetra, he failed as a noble man, but became materialistic in the quest.

When being a husband Rama failed in fulfilling in his duties, and forcing his wife into *Agniparikha,* then how come the citizens Ayodha could rely on him for justice and validation? Does the Rama's decision to command Sita to enter the fire, is held as a complete example of him being the justice giver, or maintaining peace with his subjects was more important than the household peace?

If it is held true that Sita is the ideal model for Hindu women, then it could be extended that Sita's decision to descend to the laps of mother earth is also an example to emulate. Sita's denial to accept Rama's indecisiveness and refusal to undertake the ordeal of *AgniParikha*, should also be taken as a lesson which should be imitated by women. Why that is there resides a silence on one aspect of Sita's life, while as on the other aspects there is adherence? Rama after gaining victory over the Lanka king was reunited with his wife, for whom his heart cried, but he was also a complete laid down as Rama was suspicious of Sita's chastity. The popular narrative, not only supports the fact that liberation of an ideal wife lies in her spirit to be obedient and faithful to her husband despite of any regression subjected to her but also questioning the husband is also important. Though I do accept that descending to the laps of earth is metaphoric, yet the Hindu women should seek her equality by liberating herself from the fetters of patriarchy, by starting to question the hegemonic commands that prevail in the family.

It would be wrong to comment that Sita had only been a passive victim. There are instances from the text, where she questions the authority of Rama. Though Sita has been perceived as a docile being under the commands of Rama, yet she raised her voice against the injustices, which fell into deaf ears. Soon after they went to exile, she questioned Rama on his act of attacking the demons, to save the

Brahmins. Though on the surface Sita seemed to be passive and subservient, which served as a relevant role model, but her passivity is equivocal. Madhu Kishwar comments that in comparison to Rama, Sita lies on a much higher alter. This is to say that as Rama abandoned her while she was heavily pregnant, notifies that he was not abiding by his *dharma* or duty as a husband, while as Sita always strived to adhere to her *dharma*. The resistance displayed by Sita could be well interpreted through her actions when Rama asked her to undertake a second ordeal, of trial by fire. She refused and retired to the bosom of mother earth. A throne emerges and she is swallowed by mother earth. This instance has been recorded by one of the interviewees of Kishwar as a suicide committed by Sita, in order to prove that she refuses to partake in any of Rama's fickleness.

Feminism aims at understanding the sociopolitical reality, which developed through a variety of ways: the oppression which leads to protest, legal reform, nationalist concern, education and social change. Feminism also tends to encompass identity, subject hood, space and freedom along with the recognition of the agency. Feminist thought is multifaceted which occurs in a variety of ways. If taken into account of the Indian perspectives, it questions the practices and texts, the formulated patriarchy, reinterpreted myths and tradition and focuses on a woman's body (Jain). Indian feminist argued that, culture plays a very important role which influence facets and aspects of our life. That is to say, how we react to the responses of the outside world. There lies a constant need to associate socialization of a girl to the cultural myths, which establishes the relationship between culture and self image. In a Hindu household, the women are segregated and female sexuality is 'severely repressed' (Velchura Narayan Rao).The conditions are enough ripe to protest the subverting ideology and question the role models. According to Jain, there has been an unfortunate change in female identity, which varies from Devi image to that of the public woman. The varied history of India demands that feminism is not an ideology which resists patriarchal control, but rather a movement aiming for collapsing the division between two kinds of sexuality and moral values. It aims at the distinction between "identity" and "self".

According to Thapar, mythology and historical narrative make up the historical tradition. One important aspect of *Ramayana* is that it is the brain of India. In respect to it, one can ascertain that though it is a narrative which stress on fidelity, Dharma, morality, obedience, and a relationship, yet it also encompasses fragmentation and deconstruction. The issues of sexuality and desires are equally inherent in the text. The identity of Sita is *pativrata*, but also the creation of self-was visible through her resistance. The self-images presented in the Rama*yana* are controlled by ethics, moral values, and social roles. Each character gains their status through the functioning of an agency. It is taken that patriarchy begins with the creation of myth, and hence, it can be accorded that woman has throughout the centuries have been treated as a secondary citizen, as she was born out of a male's body. The stereotypical presentation of females in the myths has led women to be inferior by birth. Sexuality has been normalized and deployed by keeping in mind the 'gender performativities' of characters in epics.

While concluding the question which remains still unanswered is that "Why there is a need of a role model"?

Hindu women are entangled in the discursive charisma
of Sita perceived as in Rama*yana*. A partial relief can
be obtained if the socialization process of a Hindu girl
is structured by keeping in mind the conflict between
'identity' and 'self'. If abiding by the Rama*yana*, is
intricately associated with the socialization of a girl child in
India, and then it is also necessary to make her realize about
rights while fulfilling her duties. It is not that by being
Sita one loss her faculty of rationality, but becomes strong
by questioning the hegemonic masculinities which are a
dominant discourse. The texts tend to present a Foucault's
argument "Power is knowledge comes true". Those who
are in power are the creators of myths and history, hence,
it is biased. The strength, diplomacy, and rationality are
evident in women characters, but always ignored and
silenced because these qualities are hegemonically attached
to men as masculine features. The narration supports that
being male encompasses being masculine, rational, logical
and protector, while as women are deemed as feminine,
dependent, followers and protected. Sita was not only
conscious about her duties were also aware of her rights.
The narrative also voices the female psychologies, through
victimization as well as resistance which help the strategic
bypassing of male control.

BIBLIOGRAPHY

Chanana, Karuna. "Hinduism and Female Sexuality: Social Control and Education of Girls in India". *Sociological Bulletin* 50.1 (2001): 37–63. Web

Ghurye, Govind Sadashiv. *The Legacy of* Rama*yana*. Bombay: Popular Prakashan, 1979. 96. Print.

Ginsburg, Faye D., Lila Abu-Lughod, and Brian Larkin. "Epic Contests Television and Religious Identity in India." *Media Worlds: Anthropology on New Terrain*. Berkeley: U of California, 2002. 134-51. Print.

Gupta, Sangeeta R.(1994). The Ambiguity of the Historical Position of Hindu Women in India: Sita, Draupadi and the Laws of Manu. *UCLA Historical Journal*.

Hess, Linda. "Rejecting Sita: Indian Responses to the Ideal Man's Cruel Treatment of His Ideal Wife." *Journal of the American Academy of Religion* 67.1 (1999): 1-32. *JSTOR*. Web. 25 Dec. 2015.

Hindery, Roderick. "Hindu Ethics in the Rāmāyana." *The Journal of Religious Ethics* 4.2 (1976): 287-322. *JSTOR*. Web. 2

Jacobs, Stephen. "Hindu Dharma in the Contemporary World: Caste, Gender and Political Hinduism." *Hinduism Today*. London: Continuum, 2010. 57-80. Print.

Jain, Jasbir. *Indigenous Roots of Feminism: Culture, Subjectivity and Agency*. New Delhi: SAGE Publications, 2011. 1. Print

Khan, Benjamin. *The Concept of Dharma in Valmiki Ramayana*. Delhi: Munshi Ram Manohar Lal, 1965. N. pag. Print.

Ramanujan, A. K. "Is There an Indian Way of Thinking? An Informal Essay." *Contributions to Indian Sociology* 23.1 (1989): 41-58. Web.

Phillip Luftengorf. "The Secret Life of Ramcandra of Ayodhya." ed. Paula Richman *Many Rāmāyaṇas: The Diversity of a Narrative Tradition in South Asia.* Berkeley: U of California, 1991. 217. Print.

Richman, Paula. "Introduction." *Many Rāmāyaṇas: The Diversity of a Narrative Tradition in South Asia.* Berkeley: U of California, 1991. N. pag. Print. Pg 3.

Richman, Paula. "Introduction." <i>Questioning Rama*yanas: A South Asian Tradition*</i>. Berkeley: U of California, 2001. N. pag. Print.

Smith, W. L. *Rāmāyaṇa Traditions in Eastern India: Assam, Bengal, Orissa.* Stockholm: Dept. of Indology, U of Stockholm, 1988, 78, Print.

Thapar, Rormila. *"Epic And History: Tradition, Dissent And Politics In India." Past and Present* 125.1 (1989): 3-26. Web

Wadley, Susan S. *"Women and the Hindu Tradition." Signs 3.1, Women and National Development: The Complexities of Change (1977)*: 113-25. *JSTOR.* Web. 25 Dec. 2015.

McLain, Karline. *India's Immortal Comic Books: Gods, Kings, and Other Heroes.* Bloomington: Indiana UP, 2009. Print.

Thapar, Romila. *Ancient Indian Social History: Some Interpretations.* New Delhi: Orient Longman, 1978. Print.

Meyer, Johann Jakob. *Sexual Life in Ancient India; a Study in the Comparative History of Indian Culture.* New York: Barnes & Noble, 1953. Print.

Scharf, Peter. *Ramopakhyana - The Story of* Rama *in the Mahabharata a Sanskrit Independent-Study Reader.* Hoboken: Taylor and Francis, 2014. Print.

Veer, Peter Van Der. *Religious Nationalism: Hindus and Muslims in India.* Berkeley, CA: U of California, 1994. Print.

Bhattacharya, Pradip. "Five Holy Virgins, Five Sacred Myths A Quest for Meaning." *Manushi* (n.d.): 4-12. Web

Chapter 13

Class consciousness and Gender discrimination in the fictions of R. K. Narayan

DR. LEENA SARKAR BHADURI
Assistant Professor
Narula Institute of Technology
81, Nilgunj Road, Agarpara,
Kolkata – 700109

I am often asked, "Where is Malgudi? All I can say is that it is imaginary and not to be found on any map...If I explain that Malgudi is a small town in South India I shall be only expressing a half truth, for the characteristics of Malgudi seem to me universal...Malgudi has been only a concept but has proved good enough for any purposes. I can't make it more concrete but has proved good enough for my purposes. I can't make it more concrete however much I might be interrogated.

R.K. Narayan, *Malgudi Days*

Malgudi is ubiquitous in all the fictions of R. K. Narayan. Socio economic and political discussions embedded in his stories are fore grounded against the backdrop of Malgudi. In the imaginary land of Malgudi Narayan explores the nuances of his creativity. The novels are not only the depictions of magical childhood but also depict social evils which bring frustration and fatigue in modern society by annihilating simplicity and happiness in human lives.

Class, Caste, Race and Gender are the social evils that have been affecting our nation for a prolonged period. Considering the nation from the pre- independence or post independence perspective, all the issues stated earlier, which were very strident and overtly expressed in the pre-independence period have now been reduced and minimised. Dissent was there in existence from the emergence of these social vices and in the post-independence period it took a concrete shape. Although the discussion strategy may foretell that the social traumas are no more in existence, but still they exist in the embedded form. Even in democratic and socialist India we still view articles in newspapers pertaining to these unhealthy practices of the society. The ostracised, traumatised, socially underprivileged classes express their deep sorrows whenever they get an opportunity to face the harsh realities of their life.

India is considered to be an abode of traditional customs and values. Class, caste, race and gender have always been the theme of different literature in vernacular or English Language. Literature reflects our culture and so literature and culture complement each other. To portray the impact of these social vices in literature, the novelist we have taken within the periphery of our discussion is R.K.Narayan. Though Narayan is acclaimed for his simplicity, readability, magnanimity but still we get an insight of some critical observations in his fictions. The background of his novels is always Malgudi, miniature India, space surrounded by tradition, culture, superstition and rigidity. Nowhere in Narayan's literary expositions have we found a vehement and vituperative attack against the social stigmas, but his reformative and rebellious attitude gradually develops in his depictions. Narayan brings in the elements of customs and conventions to captivate the Indianised ambience. A rendering of pristine human relationships, is what we discern in his novels. The artist and the visionary in Narayan obviously have a complex and non-simplistic perception of reality.

To begin with our research let us first consider the background description of his fictions. Narayan's social perception and the representation of Malgudi in his novels depict his attachment with his own community. Class, caste and race are related to social values and through series of novels Narayan clearly presents the social values, norms and mores which have been in existence and still continue to play a major role in shaping the lives of Hindu people. In this context O.P. Mathur rightly observes: 'Narayan does assert the validity of traditional Indian values but the wind from West has changed much of the panorama.'(Mathur 29) Hence the western civilization, its culture, dynamism plays an effective role to bring transfiguration in the Hindu society. This idea is contextualised in *The Vendor of Sweets* (1967) where the generational conflict between Jagan and Mali forms the theme of the novel. Mali's inclination towards America, neglecting his father's business and ideologies endorses the influx of western attitude to life. A very modern approach to life is virtually exposed by Mali when he brings a lady with him while returning from America and introduces her as his wife. The concept of 'live-in' relationship is very much westernised and dismantles the idea of divine Hindu Marriage. There is also an underlying theme of generational conflict in the emotional bond between Jagan and Mali. Mali believes in capitalism and Jagan, follower of Mahatma Gandhi believes in Sarvodaya, conflict between East and West. Narayan incorporates these issues in the novel but his concentration is to narrate the relationship between Jagan and Mali which draws the inference that he is a detached social observer. In his memoir *My Days* [1] he states the fact – he lays bare his mind in all its true spirit. His attitude to writing can be placed beside some other novelists like Defoe, Richardson and even James Joyce as these novelists keep themselves out of the purview of the action they narrate in his fictions. In this regard Allen Walter advocates:

In fact they betray their opinion on the characters and situations and – in as much as every novel is an extended metaphor of the author's view of life-on the life itself. They do so by the very choice of the characters they write about, the thoughts and feelings they give them, and the behaviour and motives they attribute to them. (Walter 16-17)

Narayan conceives the class consciousness and caste distinctions in *The Guide*, *The Bachelor of Arts* and *The Man-Eater of Malgudi*. The Guide (1958) which won for Narayan huge accolades shows the novelists's skill in placing the orient into focus for occidental eyes. Narayan depicts a comprehensive picture of human activities, the comic and the tragic, the silly and the serious, the ridiculous and the sublime. Rosie, despite being an MA in economics and a talented dancer, is abused and evicted from the patriarchal society as she hails from the class of Devdasis.[2] Just for being illegitimate she is looked down upon and categorised as a low caste. Even Marco, who willingly ties wedlock with her in spite of knowing her origin, bestows patriarchal norms on her by putting restrictions on her public performances and expects her spontaneous submissiveness in every conjugal affair. Marco symbolically represents the materialistic society where moral values are compromised for wealth and status. According to Rosie the solemnisation of her marriage is occasioned by Marco's status and position in society. Rosie says:

But all women in my family are impressed, excited that a manlike him was coming to marry one of our class, and it was decided that if it was necessary to give up our traditional art, it was worth the sacrifice. He had a big house, a motor-car, he was a man of high social standing, he had a house outside Madras, he was living in it all alone, no family at all; he lived with his books and papers. (Narayan 85)

In this context we can broadly discuss the tenets of feminist political movement which attempts to rectify sexist discrimination and social inequalities. In *The Second Sex*, Beauvoir argues- men have imagined women as the "Other", women have been denied subjectivity. Beauvoir also echoes Virginia Woolf's statement in *A Room of One's own* (1929) that women serve "as looking glasses possessing the magic and delicious power of reflecting the figure of man at twice its natural size."

In *The Bachelor of Arts* (1937) there is a mélange of western and orthodox Hindu elements. Chandran, the protagonist, in one of his solitary ramblings after passing his BA examinations, espies a girl Malathi and becomes infatuated with her. According to John Thieme: 'He is seen here as a love struck adolescent, smitten with thoughts of a girl he has barely seen and pleading with his parents to stretch the bonds of Hindu custom to allow him to marry her.' (Thieme 34) His marriage proposal with Malathi is thwarted by his orthodox and superstitious mother's belief in 'custom' and sense of low and high class. Chandran's mother dislikes the marriage proposal for her preconceived notion of class divisions in the society. She heartlessly refutes his proposal in the mere pretext of incompatible horoscopes. It brings a devastating effect in his life but ultimately he succumbs to the customs of her mother and marries the girl of their choice. The reversal of fortune is because Narayan is reluctant to speak against the social evil, although the context itself is condemning the social evil of class distinctions.

In *The Man Eater of Malgudi* (1961) a minor character Rangi, the temple dancer and the mistress of Vasu sketches the glimpse of class consciousness and its detrimental effect. Being a temple dancer she is declined social position and abhorred by every community. The traditional customs and rigidity dictates the common folk of Malgudi to segregate temple dancers from their intellectual and polished community. In *The Dark Room* Narayan provides a contrast between Savitri as a higher class woman and Ponni as a lower class woman, further clarifying Savitri's predicament. Ponni being a lower class woman is the only one in the novel who genuinely attempts to help Savitri and find a life of security and self – dependence she wants, at the same time respecting and protecting the privacy she requires. Although Ponni fights for Savitri, her sense of class consciousness initially inhibits her to take their help in life. Even after returning home, one afternoon Savitri happens to hear the tinkling sound of Mari's equipment box as he was passing by her house. Savitri attempts to break her inhibition and call him in her house to express her gratitude but society and the consciousness of high class prevents her to go further. Narayan here overwhelmingly ventilates the emotional pangs of Savitri but dares to challenge the laws imposed on society.

In the cultural topography of Malgudi these social evils play a significant role in laying the foundation of Narayan's literature. In the core of Narayan's vision and art, there lies an awareness in which the illusion and reality, the ordinary and the spiritual, the comic easily alter positions and what matters is only a change in the mode of perception. His characters make a critical survey of his epoch as they seem to give us some inkling into Narayan's political problems and institutions of his time. His 'Malgudi' epitomises the concept of global village –in the sense that our village itself embodies the entire globe.

Gender is also a crucial factor in the fictions of Narayan. It has a huge dimension and has a direct association with the feminist theory. Theoretical perceptions and analogies are not very overtly expressed in Narayan but he definitely tries to reform the position of women in Indian society and this revolution evokes the essence of feminist struggle. The episode begins with his pre-independence creations and culminates in the concept of new woman in his post-independence fictions. The word feminism refers to the advocacy of woman's right seeking to remove restrictions that discriminate against women. It relates to the belief that woman should have the same social, economic and political rights as men. Feminism has often focused upon what is absent rather than what is present, reflecting concern with marginalisation of women in patriarchal culture, a cultural organisation in the favour of men. Representation of the world like the world itself is the work of men; they describe it from their own point of view, which they confuse with absolute truth. Simon de Beauvoir[3] - Sex and gender are not, however, the only sites of women's oppressions; one can be oppressed because one is poor; one is coloured, undereducated, addicted or imprisoned. Kate Millet takes gender differences to have – 'essentially cultural, rather than biological bases.' (Millet 28-29) For her gender is 'sum total of the parents', and peers', and the culture's notions of what is appropriate to each gender by way of temperament, character, interests, status, worth, gesture, and expression.'(Millet 31) Feminine and masculine gender-norms, however, are problematic in that gendered behaviour conveniently fits with and reinforces women's subordination so that women are socialised into subordinate social roles: they learn to be passive, ignorant, docile, emotional helpmeets for men. Robbins puts feminism as - political discourses, which uncover the symptoms of oppression, whatever their grounds, diagnose the problem, and offer alternative versions of live able realities. Feminisms can also be interpreted from Indian perspective also. As the novelist under consideration is R.K.Narayan, feminism in Indian context needs to be deciphered thoroughly before delving deep into the man-woman relationships portrayed in his fictions.

From the ancient days, India was a male dominated nation with the prevalence of patriarchal[4] culture. Indian women were covered with many thick, slack layers of prejudice, convention, ignorance and reticence in literature as well as in life. Women were treated as inanimate objects, who followed five paces behind their men; they had to be gentle, docile, patient, gracious and for generations share collective responsibility in family. The term feminism in India refers to a set of movements intending to define, establish, and defend equal political, economic and social rights and equal opportunities for Indian women. Like other feminist counterparts in the world, feminists in India seek gender equality. Literary feminisms in India throw a challenge on the age long tradition of gender differentiation. It attempts to explore and find a new social order, to find pertinent resolves to the real life problems in the light of traditionally- gendered –role plays.

Narayan's novels are divided into three categories-early, middle and later novels. In his early novels –*The Dark Room* (1938) and *The English Teacher* (1945), published in the pre-independence period, the women characters are represented as orthodox and god believing entities engaged in household chores, deeply rooted to traditional beliefs, his middle novels create women who dare to pursue their own happiness escaping the noose of tradition or social portrayal of stronger and firmer female protagonist, influenced by the western philosophy and culture, and they express their resistance to male dominance, cruelty against fair sex, denial of identity and freedom of expression.

R.K.Narayan was not insensitive to female troubles and agony. It is discernible from his reminiscences on the plight of Indian women in his memoir *My Days*. He evolves a philosophy envisioning the emancipation of women which he termed as 'Women's Lib Movement'. As his memoir reveals, this philosophy was in operation while writing *The Dark Room*:

I was some how obsessed with a philosophy of woman as opposed to Man, her constant oppressor. This must have been an early testament of the "Women's Lib" movement. Man assigned her a secondary place and kept her there with such subtlety and cunning that she herself began to lose all motions of her independence, her individuality, stature and strength. A wife in an orthodox milieu of Indian society was an ideal victim of such circumstances. (Narayan 119)

The first of his novels which offers a feminist view of the contemporary South Indian society is *The Dark Room*. The dark room is actually a symbol that narrates the frustration of a perturbed, unhappy Indian wife. Savitri is portrayed with a reasonably complete picture of women 'in an orthodox milieu of Indian society', - upper caste, middle - class Malgudi, in the later 1930s. She is at first presented against her two friends Gangu and Janamma who are at the two extremes of traditional Indian society. Janamma conforms to the rule of the society: 'As for me, I have never opposed my husband or argued with him at any time in my life. I might have occasionally suggested an alternative, but nothing more. What he does is right. It is a wife's duty to feel so.'(Narayan 46) Gangu on the contrary is an eccentric, whose trendy and sophisticated husband claims to be a champion of women's rights. Savitri is positioned in between them. She is represented as a victim of the patriarchal society. Though she is dominated and neglected by her husband, like a typical Indian wife she is submissive and accepts all humiliations of her husband Ramani. When Ramani develops an illicit relationship with Shantabai, Savitri revolts against him. She vigorously exclaims: 'Don't touch me,... you are dirty, you are impure. Even if I burn my skin I can't cleanse myself of the impurity of your touch' (Narayan 87) Savitri moves out of her house, leaves her children and attempts to commit suicide. Although she is saved by a poor man but she struggles for independence and for her own identity. She struggles to get a job and earn her own livelihood. Savitri is always projected by her husband as a second and inferior category woman but her eventual revolt against Ramani brings new dimension in the novel. When she exclaims in a furious way she changes the pronoun to 'we' instead of 'I'. Savitri retorts –

Do you think I am going to stay here? We are responsible for our position: we accept food, shelter, and comforts that you give, and are what we are. Do you think that I will stay in your house, breathe the air of your property, drink the water here, and eat food you buy with your money? No, I'll starv and die in the open, under the sky, a roof for which we need to be obliged tomorrow. (Narayan 88)

The shift between 'I' and 'we' evokes the collective voice of all women who are subjected to this atrocious male domination. She fails to create her own identity as she is too powerless to subvert. Though she could not compete with her husband but it was her self- realisation and a jolt to Ramani. She returns for her emotional attachment with her children and it is not her subjugation rather she is spiritually triumphant. Two other women in the novel are also presented as socially, politically and economically independent. One is Shanta Bai who succeeds to get a job to create her own identity and the other is Pony who grabs our attention for her rebellious nature. Pony alone fights for Savitri and tries to get her job in the temple. Her spontaneous and straight forward reply to her husband and the old man of the temple reflects upon her attitude towards male fraternity. Being a low class woman she bargains ferociously with the priest when arranging an appropriate job for Savitri. Ponni can neither be intimidated by the male world nor cannot be oppressed by anyone. In this novel 'the women characters stand for a change and for resistance to change' in the words of Lakshmi Holmstrom (Srinath 7). The denouement of the novel is pessimistic as Savitri accepts defeat. It is quite evident that the liaison between Ramani and Shantabai will continue, and Savitri is too powerless to intervene again. The exploration of women's roles within marriage and their negotiation for their spaces within a patriarchal society, of course, become profoundly feminist concerns from 1930 onwards.

The next novel in our discussion is *The Guide* (1958). The novel is published in 1956, post-independence period when industrialisation and modernisation had already started blowing. Rosie belonging to an ostracized class is married to Marco. Marco disregards the desire of her instinctual self and accepts her as a commodity with no passion and emotion. He being a typical patriarch prefers his wife's confinement in the closet. He keeps himself engaged in his own career and hardly thinks about the physical demand of his wife. Rosie struggles to adjust with her destiny initially but later demonstrates the courage to move out of her unhappy conjugal life. She marries Raju, who understands her and loves her utmost. The self – realisation and rejection of gender biasness of the society where a male sex is endowed with immense freedom and female sex with no freedom at all, enunciates

Rosie's position in Indian society. Unfortunately Rosie is disillusioned later. Raju, the tourist guide, starts exploiting her, just as a money-making machine. She ponders on lost freedom and deserts Raju in fury and in a disrupted condition. Unlike Savitri of *The Dark Room* She does not go back to Marco, her first husband, instead she breaks the image of a fragile, timid Indian woman. She remains unconventional. Narayan in one of his short stories entitled 'Selvi" from the collection *An Astrologer's Day*[4], presents a similar character like Rosie. Here the story is named after the protagonist Selvi because all the events in the story, various nature of human behaviour are centered round her. Here Mohan can be compared to Raju for his monetary pursuits. Like Rosie Selvi is also considered a source of money. Mohan controls her financial matters and tries to accumulate more wealth by exploiting her talent. Selvi is benign, simple and her ignoramus appeal gives Mohan more opportunity to exploit her. Selvi is kept away from the society and almost confined in a room. He considers Selvi as his own possession. The catastrophe in his life comes when he restricts her to meet her mother as there is a hiatus of social status between Selvi and her mother. Eventually she gets the news of her demise and it brings a complete change in her life. For the first time she becomes voluble and says: 'Please leave me out of all this, leave me alone, I want to be alone hereafter. I can't bear the sight of anyone…' (Narayan164). Thus Selvi revolts against her ruthless husband and her stoic resignation shows her self – determination and mental strength. Her struggle for self – dependence is very much a feminist approach to life.

In his portrayal of self, Narayan goes the farthest in *The Painter of Signs*. Unlike Rosie who has a traditional approach to life, Daisy of *The Painter of Signs* (1977) is very much westernised. She is represented as a modern woman, who courageously chooses an unconventional profession – family planning worker. Her strong sense of individuality peeps out in all her speeches. Besides the influence of Western World due to industrialisation, there is also an East-West conflict in the characterisations of the novel. There is a tension among the three main characters- Raman, his aunt and Daisy. The tension is created by gradual disintegration of traditional values. A different type of womanhood is presented in the character of Daisy. In the words of Syed Harrex:

She employs Raman to paint propaganda signs for her de-population campaign and to accompany her to the areas where she lectures on sex education, contraception, family planning and the like while she paints slogans and signs on walls. Raman falls in love with Daisy, and then wants to marry her; she becomes ambivalently or ambiguously attracted to him, then agrees to live with him in a relationship revoking the Hindu condition of marriage but accommodating Daisy's principles of liberation and professional priorities. The essence of this situation, then, is that the old myths of arranged marriage, wifehood, and love symbolised by Sita and Radha are opposed by the new ways of modern marriage and the independent woman. (Srinath 75)

In such a situation, it is quite obvious that Raman would find himself stuck between Malgudi's conventional and outsider's iconoclasm[5], between the philosophies of the conventional woman (the aunt) and the New Woman (Daisy). In the novel Daisy is highlighted as an outsider as she does not follow conventions of the traditional Indian society and appears as an archetypal figure, a social worker and feminist to introduce Birth-Control programme top the district.

In the words of Vincent B. Leitch, "feminist theory and criticism have brought revolutionary change to literary and cultural studies by expanding the cannon, by critiquing sexist representations values, by stressing the importance of gender and sexuality, and by advocating institutional and social reforms" (Leitch 24) Adhering to this theoretical perception if we assess the contribution of Narayan's women to society then we can proclaim that they have definitely brought perceptible changes in their surrounding and in their society in general. A critical reading of all novels of R.K.Narayan will reveal the fact that he has started a movement towards the liberation of women starting from *The Dark Room* to *The Painter of Signs*. In all the novels there is one or more than one woman character who is either half way or full way of this orthodox conservative society to proclaim the right to live with self-esteem and freedom.

R.K.Narayan contextualises all the social evils in the thematic construction of his novels. He is more a worshiper of human relationships and simplicity and less a social reformer. Reformation is not vociferously instrumental in his story telling method but he incorporates society at large in a very mild tone in almost all of his literary creations. To end with the words of M.K.Bhatnagar:

Narayan is not as inclusive a chronicler of the socio-political scene as one would perhaps have in some other writers of his generation, says Bhabani Bhattacharya or Manohar Malgonkar, but it would be unfair to indict Narayan for confining himself in his novels to people whom he knows intimately- the lower middle class people, going about their lives in a well defined and graphically outlined routine. Whether one deems it a glaring weakness or an intrinsic strength of Narayan, the inescapable fact is that Narayan's world is woven round the immemorial Hindu values of patience, faith and acceptance of the morality of the individual as well as the endeavours on the part of the individual. (Bhatnagar 5)

ENDNOTES

1. In *My Days* R.K.Narayan in simple lucid style speaks of his life. The book is described in three different sections – in the first, he describes his life as a lonely child growing up in his grandmother's house in Madras; the second section deals with the obstacles he encountered as a young writer; in the last section, he gives a detailed account of his overcoming the writer's block, and the writing of *The English Teacher*.

2. 'Devdasi' is a girl dedicated to worship and service of a deity or a temple for the rest of her life. These women learned and practiced Sadir, Odissi and other forms of Classical Indian artistic tradition.

3. Simone de Beauvoir was a French writer, intellectual, existentialist philosopher, feminist and social theorist. She wrote novels, essays, biographies, an autobiography and monographs on philosophy, politics and social issues. She is best known for her novels, including *She came to Stay* and *The Mandarins*, as well as the 1949 treatise *The Second Sex*, a detailed analysis of women's oppression and a foundational tract of contemporary feminism.

4. Narayan R.K. *An Astrologer's Day and Other Stories. Mysore: Indian Thought Publication*, 1981.

5. Iconoclasm is the deliberate destruction within a culture of the culture's own religious icons and other symbols or monuments, usually for religious or political motives. It is a frequent component of major political or religious changes. The term does not generally encompass the specific destruction of images of a ruler

after his death or overthrow. People who engage in or support iconoclasm are called "iconoclasts", a term that has come to be applied figuratively to any individual who challenges established dogma or conventions.

WORKS CITED

Beauvoir Simone de. *The Second Sex*. Trans.H.m. Parshley. Vintage Books(Random House), 1989[1952].Print.

Bhatnagar M.K. "The Fictional Universe of R.K.Narayan-An Overview" in *New Insights into the novels of R.K.Narayan* edited by M.K.Bhatnagar. New Delhi: Atlantic Publishers, 2008. Print.

Harrex Syed. "R.K.Narayan: *The Painter of Signs*" in *R.K. Narayan's An Anthology of Recent Criticism* edited by C.N. Srinath. Delhi: Pencraft International, 2005. Print.

Holmstrom Lakshmi. "Women as Markers of Social Change: The Dark Room, The Guide and The Painter of Signs" in *R.K. Narayan's An Anthology of Recent Criticism* edited by C.N. Srinath. Delhi: Pencraft International, 2005. Print.

Mathur, O.P. "West Wind Blows through Malgudi" in *From Perspectives on R.K.Narayan* edited by Dr. Atma Ram. Ghaziabad: Vimal Prakashan, 1981. Print.

Millet, Kate. *Sexual Politics*. London: Granada Publishing, 1971. Print.

Narayan R.K. *The Dark Room*. Madras: Indian Thought Publication, 2009. Print.

Narayan R.K. *The Guide*. Madras: Indian Thought Publication, 2005. Print.

Narayan, R.K. *Malgudi Days*. London: Penguin, 1984. Print.

Robbins, Ruth. *Literary Feminism*. London: Macmillan, 2000. Print.

Thieme, John. *R.K.Narayan: Contemporary World Writers*. New Delhi: Viva Books Private Limited, 2010. Print.

Walter Allen. *The English Novel, Introduction.* London: Penguin International Edition, 1991.Print.

Woolf, Virginia. *A Room of One's own*, London: Cambridge University Edition, 1929. Print.

Chapter 14

Empowerment of Women through Education in India

TANUSREE SAHA
Assistant Teacher
Purapara High School (H.S.),
Murshidabad, West Bengal

INTRODUCTION

Women constitute almost half of the population in our country. So, for human development, empowerment of women gains priority. Women need to be empowered socially, economically and politically. Education is the key factor for women empowerment, prosperity, development and welfare.

EDUCATION FOR WOMEN'S EQUALITY: NATIONAL POLICY ON EDUCATION

The NPE (1986 and as modified in 1992) has made the following observations in Part III in Paras 4.2 and 4.3 under the Theme 'Education for Women's Equality.

4.2 Education will be used as an agent of basic charge in the status of women. In order to neutralize the accumulated distortions of the past there will be a conceived edge in favour of women. The National Education System will play a positive, interventionist role in the development of women. It will foster the development of new values through redesigned curricula, textbooks, the training and orientation of teachers, decision makers and administrators and the active involvement of educational institutions. This will be an act of faith and social engineering. Women studies will be promoted as a part of various courses and educational institutions encouraged to take up active programmes to further Women's development.

4.3: The removal of women's illiteracy and obstacles inhibiting their access to, and retention in, elementary education will receive over-riding priority, through provision for social support services, setting of time targets, and effective monitoring. Major emphasis will be laid on women's participation in vocational, technical and professional education at different levels. The policy of non-discrimination will be pursued vigorously to eliminate sex stereotyping in vocational and professional courses and to promote Women's participation in non-traditional occupations, as well as in existing and emergent technologies.

Table 21.1: Selected Gender Development Indicators: 1981 to 2001

Sl. No.	Indicator	Women	Men	Total	Women	Men	Total
(1)	(2)	(3)	(4)	(5)	(6)	(7)	(8)
Demography and Vital Statistics							
1.	Population (in million in 1981 & 2001)	330.0	353.4	683.4	495.7	531.3	1027.0
2.	Decennial Growth (1981 & 2001)*	24.93	24.41	24.66	21.79	20.93	21.34
3.	Sex Ratio (1981 & 2001) **	934	--	--	933	--	--
4.	Life Expectancy at Birth (in years in 1981-85 & 1996-01)	55.7	55.4	--	65.3	62.3	--
5.	Mean Age at Marriage (in years in 1981 & 1991)	18.3	23.3	--	19.5	23.9	--

Health & Family welfare									
6.	Birth Rate (per thousand in 1981 & 1999)	--	--	33.9	--	--	--	26.1
7.	Death Rate (per thousand in 1981 & 1999)	12.7	12.4	12.5	8.3	9.0	8.7
8.	Infant Mortality Rate (per thousand live births in 1988 & 1999)	93.0	96.0	94.5	70.8	69.8	70.0
9.	Child Mortality Rate (per thousand live births under 5 years of age in 1985 & 1997)	40.4	36.6	--	24.5	21.8	--
10.	Maternal Mortality Rate (Per one lakh live births in 1980 & 1998)	468	--	--	407	--	--

Literacy and Education							
11.	Literacy Rates (1981 & 2001)*	29.75	56.38	43.57	54.16	75.85	65.38
12.	Gross Enrolment Ratio (1980-81 & 1999-2000)						
	- Classes –I – V	64.1	95.8	80.5	85.2	104.1	94.9
	- Classes VI-VIII	28.6	54.3	41.9	49.7	67.2	58.8
13.	Drop-out Rate (1980-81 & 1999-2000)						
	- Classes –I – V	62.5	56.2	58.7	42.3	38.7	40.3
	- Classes VI-VIII	79.4	68.0	72.7	58.0	52.0	54.6
Work and Employment							
14.	Work Participation Rate (1981 & 2001)*	19.7	52.6	36.7	25.7	51.9	39.3
15.	Organised Sector (No. in million in 1981 & 1999)	2.80	20.05	22.85	4.83	23.28	28.11
		(12.2%)			(17.2%)		

16.	Public Sector (No. in million in 1984 & 1999)	1.5 (9.7%)	14.0	15.5	2.8 (14.5%)	16.6	19.4
17.	Government (No. in million in 1981 & 1997)	1.2 (11%)	9.7	10.9	1.6 (14.6%)	9.1	10.7
Decision-Making							
18.	Administration (No. in IAS & IPS in 1978 & 2000)	360 (5.4%)	6262	6622	645 (7.6%)	7815	8460
19.	PRIs (No. in thousand in 1995 & 2001)	318*** (33.5%)	630888	948***	725 (26.6%)	1997	2722
20.	Parliament (No. 1998 & 2001)	59 (7.2%)	761	820	70 (8.5%)	750	820
21.	Central Council of Ministers (No. in 1985 & 2001)	4 (10%)	36	40	8 (10.8%)	66	74

- Figures in percent ** females per 1,000 males; *** Refers to 1995 in respect of some States, namely, Gujarat, Haryana, Karnataka, Kerala, Madhya Pradesh, Punjab, Rajasthan, Tripura and West Bengal.

Note: (i) Figures in parentheses indicate the percentage to the total and year of the data in respective columns. Although, efforts were made to keep a common 'base' and common 'comparable year', but the same could not be kept up because of the limitations in the availability of data and other practical problems. (ii) The years given in the parentheses refer to the year of the data in columns 3.4 & 5 and 6, 7 & 8 respectively.

Sources: 1. Census of India, 1991, Census of India, 2001; Provisional Population Totals: and SRS Bulletins for respective years, Registrar General & Census Commissioner. GOI. New Delhi; 2. Selected Educational Statistics for respective years. Dept of Education, Ministry of HRD, New Delhi; 3 Annual Report, 1999-200, Dept of Elementary & Literacy and Secondary & Higher Education, Ministry of HRD, New Delhi; 4. Employment Exchange Statistics, DGE & T. Ministry of Labour, New Delhi; 5. Dept of Personnel & Training, New Delhi, 6. Ministry of Rural Development, New Delhi; 7. Election Commission of India, New Delhi; 8. National Informatics Centre Parliament House, New Delhi.

Table 21.2: Gross Enrolment Rates of Girls /
Secondary Classes Since Independence.

Year	Girls	Total
1950-51	17.7	32.1
1960-61	30.9	48.7
1970-71	44.4	61.9
1980-81	52.1	67.5
1990-91	70.8	86.0
2000-2001	72.4	87.0

Table 21.3: Women Enrolment and Total Enrolment in Higher
Education in Universities and Colleges (1995-96 to 2001-2002)

Year	Total Enrolment	Women Enrolment	Women Percentage
1995-96	65,74,005	23,63,607	36
1996-97	68,42,598	25,14,511	37
1997-98	72,60,418	27,22,062	37
1998-99	77,05,520	29,32,993	38
1999-2000	80,50,607	31,12,090	39
2000-2001	83,99,443	33,06,410	39.4
2001-2002	88,21,095	35,14,450	39.84

LIFE-CYCLE APPROACH TO EMPOWERMENT OF WOMEN

Empowering women as a process demands a life-cycle approach. Therefore, every stage of their life counts as a priority in the planning process. Depending upon the development needs at every stage, female population has been categories into 5 district sub-groups (population as projected for 2001). They include:

- Girl children in the age-group 0-14 years who account for 171.50 million (34.6 percent), deserve special attention because of the gender bias and discrimination they suffer from at such a tender age;
- Adolescent girls in the age-group 15-19 years who account for 52.14 million (10.5 per cent) are very sensitive from the view-point of planning because

of the preparatory stage for their future productive and reproductive roles in the society and family, respectively.

- Women in the reproductive age-group 15-44 years numbering 233.72 million (47.1 percent) need special care and attention because of their reproductive needs.

- Women in the economically active age-group 15-59 years, who account for 289.40 million (58.4 percent), have different demands like those of education / training, employment, income generation and participation in the developmental process, decision making etc. and.

- The elderly women in the age-group 60+ years numbering 34.87 million (7.0 percent), have limited needs mainly relating to health, financial and emotional support.

SPECIAL INITIATIVES / ACHIEVEMENTS FOR THE EMPOWERMENT OF WOMEN DURING THE NINTH PLAN (1997-2002)

- Adoption of Women's Component Plan (WCP) to ensure that benefits from other developmental sectors do not by-pass women and not less than 30 percent of funds / benefits flow to them from all the women related sectors. Review of the progress of WCP during the Ninth Plan reveals that funds flowing from one of the women-related Departments (viz. Family Welfare) was as high as 70 percent of its Gross Budgetary Support of the Ninth Plan (1997).

- Launching of 'Swa-Shakti' to create an enabling environment for empowerment of women through setting up of self-reliant Self-Help Groups (SHGs) and developing linkages with lending institutions to ensure women's access to credit facilities for income-generation activities (1998).

- Stree Shakti Puraskars' instituted for the first time in the history of women's development to honour 5 distinguished women annually for their outstanding contribution to the upliftment and empowerment of women; (1999).

- Setting up of a Task Force on Women under the Chairpersonship, Deputy Chairman, Planning Commission to review the existing women specific and women-related legislations and suggest enactment of new legislations or amendments, wherever necessary. The Task Force also suggested a thematic programme for celebrating the year 2001 as Women's Empowerment Year, besides reviewing 22 existing legislations; (2000).

- Introduction of Gender Budgeting to attain more effective targeting of public expenditure and to offset any undesirable gender-specific consequences of previous budgetary measures; (2000-01).

- Adoption of a National Policy for Empowerment of Women to eliminate all types of discrimination against women and to ensure gender justice, besides empowering women both socially and economically; (2001).

- Celebration of the year 2001 as 'Women's Empowerment Year' to create awareness generation, remove negative thinking, besides building up confidence in women through the processes of conscientization so that they can take their rightful place in the mainstream of the nation's social political and economic life; (2001).

- Recasting of Indira Mahila Yojana as 'Swayamsidha', and intergatory programme for empowerment of women through a major strategy converging the servies available in all the women-related programme besides organizing women into SHGs for undertaking various entrepreneurial ventures; (2001).
- Launching of 'Swadhar' to extend rehabilitation services for 'Women' in Difficult Circumstances'; (2001).
- Introduction of a Bill on Domestic Violence against Women (Prevention) to eliminate all forms of domestic violence against women and the girl child; (2002).

Four fold strategy for Empowerment of Women during the Tenth Plan

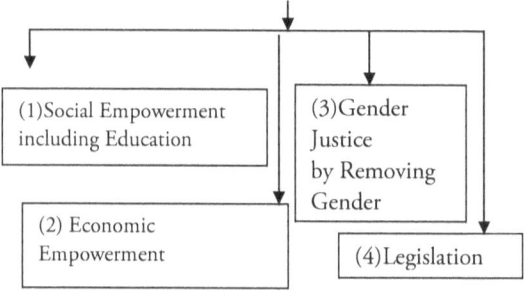

(1)Social Empowerment including Education

(2) Economic Empowerment

(3)Gender Justice by Removing Gender

(4)Legislation

TENTH FIVE YEAR PLAN (2002-2007)

ECONOMIC EMPOWERMENT OF WOMEN

Ensure provision of training, employment and income generation activities with both 'forward' and 'backward' linkages with the ultimate objective of making all women economically independent and self-reliant through –

- Organising women into Self-Help Groups under various poverty alleviation programmes, viz. Swarnajayanti Gram Swarozger Yojana (SGSY), Swarna Jayanti Shahri Rozar Yojana (SJSRY), Rashtriya Mahila Kosh (RMK), Support for Training and Employment Programme (STEP), Training-cum-Production Centres for Women (NORAD) etc and offering them a range of economic options along with necessary support measures to enhance their capabilities and earning capacities with an ultimate objective of making them economically independent and self-reliant.
- Ensuring that women in the Informal Sector who account for more than 90 percent are given special attention with regard to improving their working conditions as the same continued to be very precarious without even minimum or equal wages, leave aside other legislative safeguards.
- Making concerted efforts to ensure that the benefits of training and extension in agriculture and its allied activities of horticulture, small animal husbandry, poultry, fisheries, etc. reach women in proportion to their numbers; and also

issue of joint Pattas for husband and wife under
the Social Forestry and Joint Forest Management
programmes.

- Ensuring that the employers fulfill their legal
obligations towards their women workers in
extending child care facilities, maternity benefits,
special leave, protection from occupational hazards,
allowing formation of women workers' associations
/ unions, legal protection / aid etc.

- Re-training / upgrading the skills of women
displaced from traditional sectors due to
advancement of technology so that they can
take up jobs in the new and expanding areas
of employment and formulating appropriate
policies and programmes to promote alternative
opportunities for wage / self-employment in
traditional sectors like khadi and village industries,
handicrafts, handlooms, sericulture, small scale
and cottage industries.

- Initiating affirmative action to ensure at least 30
percent of reservation for women in services in the
Public Sector as their representation in 1999 was
only 14.5 percent, along with required provisions
for upward mobility.

- Increasing access to credit for women either through
the establishment of new micro-credit mechanisms
or micro-financial institutions catering to women
or strengthening existing arrangements in these
areas along with an expansion of the limited
coverage of RMK.

SOCIAL EMPOWERMENT (INCLUDING EDUCATION OF WOMEN)

Creating an enabling environment through adopting various affirmative developmental policies and programmes for development of women, besides providing them easy and equal access to all the basic minimum services so as to enable them to realize their full potentials through.

Providing easy and equal access to ensure basic minimum services of primary health care and family welfare with a special focus on the under-served and under-privileged segments of population through universalizing Reproductive and Child Health (RCH) services.

- Achieving the goals set by the National Population Policy (2000) with regard to reducing Infant Mortality Rate (IMR) to 30 per thousand and Maternal Mortality Rate (MMR) to 100 per lakh live births by 2010.
- Supplementing health care and nutrition services through the Pradhan Mantri Gramodaya Yojana (PMGY) to fill the critical gaps in the existing primary health care infrastructure and nutrition services.
- Tackling both macro and micro-nutrient deficiencies through nutrition supplementary feeding programmes with necessary support services like health check-ups, immunization, health and nutrition education and nutrition awareness etc.
- Consolidating the progress made under female education and carrying it forward for achieving

the set goal of 'Education for Women's Equality' as advocated by the National Policy of Education, 1986 (revised in 1992).

- Providing easy and equal access to and free education for women and girls at all levels and in the field of technical and vocational education and training in up-coming and job-oriented trades.
- Increasing enrolment / retention rates and reducing drop-out rates by expanding the support services through mid-day meals, hostels and incentives like free supply of uniforms, textbooks, transport charges etc.
- Extending the existing network of regional vocational training centres to all the states and Women's Industrial Training Institutes and Women's Wings with General Industrial Training Institutes with residential facilities in all districts and sub-districts and provision of training in marketable trades.
- Encouraging the media to project positive images of women and the Girl Child; change the mind-set of the people and thus promote the balanced portrayals of women and men.
- Gender sensitizing both the administrative and enforcement machinery and ensuring that the rights and interests of women are taken care of, besides involving them in planning, implementation and monitoring of processes.

GENDER JUSTICE BY REMOVING GENDER DISCRIMINATION

Eliminate all forms of gender discrimination and, thus, enable women to enjoy not only de-jure but also de-facto rights and fundamental freedom on par with men in all spheres, viz. political, economic, social, civil, cultural etc. through –

- Complete eradication of female foeticide and female infanticide through effective enforcement of both the Indian Penal Code, 1860 and the Pre-Natal Diagnostic Technique (Regulation and Prevention of Misuse) Act, 1994 with most stringent measures of punishment so that a very harsh path is set for the illegal practitioners.
- Adopting measures that take into account the reproductive rights of women to enable them to exercise their reproductive choices.
- Working out strategies, in close collaboration with the Ministry of Labour, to ensure extension of employment opportunities and thus, remove inequalities in employment – both in work and accessibility.
- Initiating interventions at the macro-economic level to amend existing legislations to improve women's access to productive assets and resources.
- Ensuring that the value added by women in the Informal Sector as workers and producers is recognized through redefinition / re-interpretation of conventional concepts of work and preparation of Satellite and National Accounts.

- Defining the Women's Component Plan (WCP) clearly and identifying the schemes / programmes / projects under each Ministry / Department which should be covered under WCP and ensuring the adoption of women-related machanisms through which funds / benefits flow to women from these sectors.

- Initiating action for enacting new women-specific legislations; amending the existing women-related legislation, if necessary, based on the review made and recommendations already available to ensure gender justice, besides, reviewing all the subordinate legislations to eliminate all gender discriminatory references.

- Expending action to legislate reservation of not less than 1/3 seats for women in the Parliament and in the State Legislative Assemblies and thus ensures women in proportion to their numbers reach decision making bodies so that their voices are heard.

- Arresting the ever-increading violence against women and the Girl Child including the Adolescent girls on top priority with the strength and support of a well-planned Programme of Action prepared in consultation with all the concerned, especially the enforcement authorities; implementing effectively with the strength of the Law and Order Authorities both at the centre and state levels and assessing the situation.

- Expending standardization of a Gender Development Index based on which the gender segregated data will be collected at national, state and district levels; compiled / collated and analyzed to assess the progress made in improving the status of women at regular intervals with an ultimate objective of achieving equality on par with men.

- Initiating / accelerating the process of societal reorientation towards creating a Gender-Just Society.

LEGISLATIVE SUPPORT FOR WOMEN

WOMEN-SPECIFIC LEGISLATIONS

- The Immoral Traffic (Prevention) Act, 1956*
- The Dowry Prohibition Act. 1961 (28 of 1961)*
- The Indecent Representation of Women (Prohibition) Act, 1986*
- The Commission of Sati (Prevention) Act, 1987 (3 of 1988)*

WOMEN-RELATED LEGISLATIONS

- The Guardians and Wards Act, 1860 (8 of 1890)*
- Indian Penal Code, 1860**
- The Christian Marriage Act, 1872 (15 of 1872)*
- The Indian Evidence Act, 1872 (yet to be reviewed)
- The Married Women's Property Act, 1874 (3 of 1874)*
- The Workmen's Compensation Act, 1923**
- The Legal Practitioners (Women) Act, 1923*
- The Indian Succession Act, 1925 (39 of 1925)*

- The Child Marriage Restraint Act, 1929 (19 of 1929)*
- The Payments of Wages Act, 1936**
- The Muslim Personal Law (Shariat) Application Act, 1937*
- The Factories Act, 1948*
- The Minimum Wages Act, 1948*
- The Employees' State Insurance Act, 1948*
- The Plantation Labour Act, 1951**
- The Cinematograph Act, 1952**
- The Special Marriage Act, 1954*
- The Hindu Marriage Act, 1955 (28 of 1989)*
- The Hindu Adoptions & Maintenance Act. 1956*
- The Hindu Minority & Guardianship Act, 1956*
- The Hindu Succession Act, 1956*
- The Maternity Benefit Act, 1961 (53 of 1961)*
- The Beedi & Cigar Workers (Conditions of Employment) Act, 1966
- The Foreign Marriage Act, 1969 (33 of 1969)*
- The Indian Divorce Act, 1969 (4 of 1969)*
- The Medical Termination of Pregnancy Act, 1971
- (34 of 1971)*
- Code of Criminal procedure, 1973**
- The Bonded Labour System (Abolition) Act, 1976*
- The Equal Remuneration Act, 1976*
- The Contract Labour (Regulation & Abolition) Act, 1979.
- The Inter-State Migrant Workmen (Regulation of Employment and Conditions of Service) Act, 1979*
- The Family Courts Act, 1984*
- Juvenile Justice Act, 1986*

- The Child Labour (Prohibition & Regulation) Act, 1986**
- National Commission for Women Act, 1990 (20 of 1990)*
- The Infant Milk Substitutes, Feeding Bottles and Infant Foods (Regulation of Production, Supply and Distribution) Act, 1992*
- The Pre-Natal Diagnostic Technique (Regulation and Prevention of Misuse) Act. 1994*

* Reviewed by National Commission for Women (NCW)
** Reviewed by the Task Force on Women & Children.
@ Reviewed by both NCW and the Task Force on Women & Children.

CONCLUSION

There is continued inequality and vulnerability of women in India in all sectors Economic, Education, Social, Political, Health care, Nutrition, Right and Legal etc. Women oppressed in all spheres of life, they need to be empowered in all walk of life. In order to swim against the system the requires more strength. Such strength comes from the process of empowerment and empowerment will come from the education. And rural development will come from women empowerment. Education is milestone of women empowerment because it enables them to responds to the challenges to confront their traditional role and change their life. Education helps women to be empowered socially, economically and politically.

REFERENCES

- J.C. Agarwal – Development of Education System in India.
- Anita Arya – Indian Women Education and Empowerment.
- G.B. Reddy – Women and the Law
- J.C. Agarwal – Development and planning of Modern Education.
- Mira Seth – Women and Development. The India Experience.
- Sukanya Nihal Singh – Prospect for Women Empowerment.

Chapter 15

Sexuality in Egyptian Society: Feminist Reading of Rifaat's Short Stories

AMRITA BASU ROY CHOWDHURY
Senior Research Fellow
School of Women's Studies
Jadavpur University

Jessica Ellen Cornish (born 27 March 1988), an English pop singer and songwriter, better known by her stage name Jessie J, once in an interview conducted by BBC News mentioned:

"I want women to know that they can belong - whatever your culture, your religion, your sexuality - that you can live life how you want to live it and feel comfortable how you are."

Perhaps, Fatimah Rifaat (1930 –1996), more famous by her pen name Alifa Rifaat, endeavoured to communicate the same message through her writings. Alifa Rifaat's writings are vociferous outbursts of the silent women, who are taught to abide and who follow certain patriarchal traditions and customs - sometimes because out of their fear of being outcast and punished, sometimes because they don't have choices to make or sometimes simply because they consider these traditions and practices sacrosanct as they are unaware of any other ways of cultural or social life. However, in all of the above cases, somewhere the concept of establishing the identity of being a 'woman' is lost, somewhere behind all these 'purdahs' of culture, the hidden and unspoken desires of women are compromised. A common theme that runs through Rifaat's works is the mistreatment of women by men, fellow women and the society. For dealing with these issues, death, frustrations and changes have been used as the vehicle through which these stories are told. As a Muslim, Alifa Rifaat speaks not against the dictates of the *Quran*, as the 'call to prayer' was a phrase that was used in almost all the stories. What Alifa seeks to do is to address the issue of human interpretation and misinterpretation of this sacred book, and how these interpretations have been aligned and modified, practiced and passed on for ages in our societies to benefit individuals with superior gender roles and consequently, have contributed in establishing a biased patriarchal society. Alifa Rifaat's works signify the position and status of women in Muslim society and the problems inherent in a patriarchal society where men do not adhere to their religious teachings that advocate just treatment to women belonging to Muslim community. To validate, I'm quoting renowned scholar Ramzi M. Salti's observation from his article 'Feminism and Religion in Alifa Rifaat's Short Stories':

"Muslim authors such as Alifa Rifaat and Nawal Sadaawi have fought largely for an independent identity for women within the context of Islam, without adopting a secular view or one which deviates from certain accepted social norms. Such authors, of course, hold the view that there indeed is a dignified and independent place for women within Islam, provided that the *Quranic* teachings on women are followed more faithfully."

Before entering into the domain of the discussion let us glance through a few significant facts about Rifaat very quickly. Fatimah Abdullah Rifaat was born in 1930 in Cairo to a well-to-do architect and his wife and was brought up in the Islamic tradition, procuring a deeper understanding of the tradition comparatively at an early age.

Rifaat began writing after her marriage and published a short story in 1955 as Alifa Rifaat, a pseudonym she used until 1960. When her husband demanded she immediately stopped writing. For more than a decade, she conformed to his wishes, during which time she fervently studied literature, science, astronomy, and history. After severe illness in 1973, her husband allowed her to resume her writing. Beginning in 1974, a number of short stories were published in a literary journal, followed by a collection of short stories, Eve Returns with Adam to Paradise (1975), and a novel, The Jewel of Pharo (1978). She continued to publish short stories through the 1980s following the death of her husband. During the next six years, Rifaat published more than ninety short stories in various Egyptian journals and magazines, and in 1981 published another collection of stories titled Who is Man?, a book that proved so controversial that it was not sold in most Egyptian bookstores. Rifaat, whose works until that point of time were mostly overlooked by the intellectuals of the society, perceived herself as the target of religious fundamentalists and orthodox critics who considered certain issues in her stories (for example, lesbianism, female sexual desire, rape and so on) too obscene or too contradictory to the existing social norms in the Arab world. Fortunately there was other group of critics who appreciated the new Rifaat, and reviews of her works by certain Arab and Western critics proved quite boosting for the author. In 1983, Rifaat published a new collection of stories which she called Prayer of Love. In 1985 In the Long Winter Night was published. Meanwhile Rifaat in 1984 won the Excellence Award from the Modern Literature Assembly. She had gifted her readers with nearly one hundred short stories to Arabic and English magazines, and her work was also produced for television. Her novel Girls of Baurdin was published in 1995.

The short story genre for Rifaat became a strategy of conveying an Egyptian woman's culturally and socially constructed diurnal life. Many of Rifaat's short stories have invited controversies and criticisms throughout the Arab world, triggering discontent and revulsion among many religious leaders as well as other authors. This reaction is predominant when one breaks away the accepted norms in a society. Rifaat was not an exception in this case. Like others her works were also being evaluated from patriarchal subjective position rather than from an objective perspective. But there were a few who endorsed her potential. To validate I'm quoting:"Not only was Rifaat's works ahead of its time for Arab women's writing in addressing the subject of women's bodies, but it was recognized in Western academic circles as well. Rifaat's works also reflect a social conflict over the women's body during an era of polarization in Egypt (1970s-1980s). It is this conflict between the extremist radical rhetoric and openness to Western cultures that lies behind many of the contradictions in tone within Rifaat's narratives."[14]

Distant View of a Minaret, published in 1983, is one of her best known works in English. It is a collection of fifteen short stories that give readers a glimpse of what it means to be a woman in an orthodox Muslim society in Egypt. The stories address different issues like pre-marital sex, unfulfilled sexual desire, identity crisis, gender discrimination, the loneliness as a consequence of being a 'woman' and so on which are very much attuned to women's life in a male dominated society. For this particular paper I will be concentrating on two stories of the collection- the title story 'Distant View of a Minaret' & 'Bahiyya's Eyes' which mostly focus on how the notion of sexuality is being bestowed upon women in Egyptian society.

Before I step into the discussion I would like to outline the theme of the title story 'Distant View of a Minaret'. As the story opens we find a woman and her husband, having sexual intercourse. The wife ponders over the lack of her sexual satisfaction. Her husband always withdraws as soon as he climaxes. Though she tries to communicate her sexual need, he flouts her and gives her a sense of embarrassment for trying to prolong the entire process of sexual intercourse in order to have an orgasm. As the story proceeds, the wife hears the call for prayer. She gets up to clean herself after sexual interaction, in keeping with Islamic practice. Her husband remains asleep. After prayer, the wife stares out the window of their apartment, reminiscing that she once had a spectacle of the entire city of Cairo. The city has

---

[14] Gul Ozyegin (Ed.), *Gender and Sexuality in Muslim Culture*, USA, Ashgate Publishing House, 1998, p. 282.

expanded over the years, and now the view is confined to that of a single minaret that is the tower of a mosque. She had aspired to have a house with a garden in the suburbs. Because of her husband's job, they bought an apartment in the city. She was not unhappy to stay there because of the wonderful view of the city Cairo, although it has lost its beauty gradually.

The wife later prepares the afternoon coffee and brings it into the bedroom for her husband. Suddenly she discovers that her husband is too cold to move. She guesses the truth. She tells her son to fetch the doctor, and then pours a cup of coffee for herself. It seems that she is surprisingly calm after her husband's death. Instead of mourning, a sense of numbness engulfs her. Here I would like to refer to a Bengali film titled, Paromitar Ekdin (2000) where a similar kind of situation takes place. Sanaka, one of the protagonists of the film, never seems happy with her married life. Her husband is ignorant of his wife's needs-either sexual or mental or physical. Sanaka, however, takes sincere care of the entire family comprising of her husband, two sons, daughters- in- law, grandson, granddaughter and her only daughter, Khuku, who is mentally challenged. Sanaka tries to find solace by watching Bengali serials and movies. From the onset we find Sanaka's husband constantly dictating his wife although Sanaka retains her own standpoint. One afternoon while taking lunch with her family members, she receives the news of her husband's demise. Paromita embraces her expecting that she will burst into tears, however, Sanka's reaction was otherwise; she remains indifferent and unaffected with a blank and vacant look on her face, finishes the last morsel of meal and continues with the daily chores. Here lies the analogy between the lady in 'Distant View of a Minaret' and Sanaka in Paromitar Ekdin. Both these characters, denied of their sexual desire and subject to ignorance and dominance from their husbands, do not reflect any emotional turmoil but turn unresponsive on their demise.

Coming back to 'Distant View of a Minaret', it seems that religious activities, to which the wife staunchly abides by, provided her with a sense of relief and peace, which her husband, even after their long years of marriage and apparent togetherness, could not provide her. Therefore, somewhere deep within, he turns into an individual whose presence or absence has no significant psychological impact in her life, a husband whose 'existence' or 'death' seems meaningless to her. To justify I'm quoting from the text:

"Her five daily prayers were like punctuation marks that divided up and gave meaning to her life. But how would a woman who has been sex-starved since the beginning of her marriage feel when the husband dies?"

The title story 'Distant view of a minaret' is an unusually constructed piece of narrative in which the 'Muslim Concept of Active Female Sexuality' is played out in a dramatic mode. Tellingly unnamed, the female character remembers her frantic attempts to make her husband feel her sexual needs. Her incompetence to openly discuss her wishes with her husband points to a code of silence by which sexual matters between them remain a forbidden, an un-trodden subject. This silence blanketing the subject of sex gives birth to a gap between male-female relationships. Even married women in Egyptian society talk about their sexual relationships with their husbands in hushed terms. Therefore, the female character is stuck in a situation where she can neither express her wishes and desires to her husband or to her female friends. In an endeavour to get rid of this hurdle she possibly chooses to express her needs through body language, "but on each occasion, when breathlessly imploring him to continue, he would – as though purposely to deprive her – quicken his movements and bring the act to an abrupt end". Being unsuccessful to communicate her need by action, the character in due course gives up and succumbs to an indifferent, indolent role, which endorses her husband's absolute control over their sexual entity. Thus, her sexual desire becomes passive not by choice but through the forceful, egoistic act of her husband.

In a revised edition of her book *Beyond the Veil: Male-Female Dynamics in Modern Muslim Society* the Moroccan sociologist Fatima Mernissi explains that "what Muslim theory considers destructive to the social order is *active female sexuality* rather than *sexuality* itself, for while sexuality per se is not a danger, the woman is *fitna*–a living representative of the dangers of sexuality and its rampant disruptive potential". Thus, to maintain the social order, female sexuality has to be subdued, if not absent. Rifaat in 'Distant view of a Minaret' projects how male agency is contributing to this process. The protagonist's husband does not only fail to reciprocate her sexual needs but also fails to comprehend that the needs even exist. The significance of the title of the story surfaces as the female character sits near a window after the sexual act and looks out at the city of Cairo. She observes that Cairo, which used to have countless mosques and minarets, now has only the single visible minaret, "the tall solitary minaret that could be seen between two towering blocks of flats". She notes that "this single minaret, one of the twin minarets of the Mosque of Sultan Hasan, with above it a thin slice of the Citadel, was all that was now left of the panoramic view she had once had of old Cairo". The solitary minaret is a symbol of the female character herself, a lonely, unhappy woman in an unfulfilled marriage, who is caught between two overpowering blocks: a patriarchal culture which inhibits woman's sexuality, on the one hand, and woman's desire to be sexually fulfilled, on the other. This juxtaposition brings out the contrast between male attitudes toward women's sexuality and women's right to loving and kind treatment in marriage as prescribed by the *Quran*. Thus, this construction of woman by Rifaat upholds two very disturbing and dichotomous scenarios; on one hand we have the strong patriarchal elements and patronisers of Islam, who may have interpreted and practiced their religious doctrines to their own advantage, or may have unknowingly misinterpreted Islam anyways, but are unable to provide solace, peace and tranquillity to a woman who practices the same religion. On the other hand, the woman in context finds solace when she fulfils her practices of the same religion and attributes them to provide meanings in her life. Maybe for this woman, the 'minaret' is the place where this dichotomy of the society and her own disturbances can be put to rest; maybe the 'minaret' or her religion has all the answers. Maybe that is why, even after the city of Cairo is now changed with new structures, the 'minaret' is the only structure that stands tall and catches her eyes.

Coming to the second story of my discussion, 'Bahiyya's Eyes' is a deeply moving story that narrates different problems affecting a woman's life such as female genital mutilation, men controlling female sexuality, the choosing of husbands and so on. It is a painful narration of an old woman to her daughter about the struggles she has endured. The narration includes her trauma and her sense of stigma that followed after she was caught having moulded male and female clay models with their private parts intact:

"…they took hold of me and forced my legs and cut away the mulberry with a razor. They left me with a wound in my body and another wound deep inside me, a feeling that a wrong has been done to me, a wrong that could never be undone."

In 'Bahiyya's Eyes', while conversing with her daughter, Bahiyya meticulously sums up the way she perceives the role of women, emphasizing the fact that in a patriarchal society "A man's still a man and a woman will remain a woman whatever she does… Daughter, I'm not crying now because I'm fed up or regret that the Lord created me a woman … It's just that I'm sad about my life and youth that have come and gone without my knowing how to live them really and truly as a woman". Basically the sexist practices are being entrenched in patriarchy by institutional and social application of those practices. But these practices cannot be easily recognized as they are naturalized within the system. 'Patriarchy' refers to a society, system or country that is ruled or controlled by men. Patriarchy assigns different roles to men and women to perform and it tends to objectify the role of women. But this objectification varies from one culture to another, from one period of history to another. What is common and central to all forms of patriarchy is male dominance. It asserts a power relation where women are placed in the periphery and men in the core. To validate my point I'm quoting Shefali Moitra:

"Patriarchy is necessarily related to power. Those who have power have right to control the destiny of those who are powerless-it works on the principle that 'superiority justifies domination'. Patriarchy necessarily incorporates and sanctions an unequal distribution of power which helps maintain the status quo of oppression." It seems that patriarchy privileges man with his gender role whereas it subjugates woman assigning an inferior gender role to perform within the system.

It seems that Bahiyya accepts her fate as a woman. She is never willing to change her life nor does she try to revolt against the patriarchal norms of the society. Her life, which she describes thoroughly to her daughter, seems at first glimpse to be nothing more than a series of endless painful occurrences and torture. Therefore, her life is devoid of any contentment or happiness. During the course of her conversation, she mentions how she was beaten by her brother, how the sexual domination was exercised by her husband after her arranged marriage, and how brutally she faced her puberty in early stages without prior knowledge or support from her mother or anyone else. Still, beneath this apparent sad saga of her life, or as Miriam Cooke coins it, "the painful drudgery that only fantasy can render tolerable", Bahiyya, however, indicates the possibility of joy for a woman in her condition, even under the repressive environments that have always engulfed her life. She mentions, for instance, that "of course the whole of life wasn't all misery" since amidst the chaotic ambience she managed to have special moments. There she experienced a feeling which she narrates as coming close to ecstasy and satisfaction. Expectedly, these moments ensued when she was alone with nature, far away from the madding crowd, when she would "sit down and play alongside the water channel and make things out of mud and leave them in the sun to dry. Another fond memory that Bahiyya recalls, took place at a later stage of her life when she found herself in love for the first time with a man who reciprocated her with love and care. Having lived through a depressing, unhappy childhood, Bahiyya immediately sees in this man 'the redeemer' she had long craved for and she describes the nights she had spent dreaming of him in order to assure herself "that this was the man who'd make (*her*) feel glad that (*she*) was born a woman". It is no miracle then that she paradoxically experiences soon after that "there's no happier time for a girl than when her heart's still green and full of hope".

It is noteworthy to mention that even in 'Bahiyya's Eyes', the culpability for women's situation in parts of Egypt is never directed towards God or Islam. Rifaat does not blame the Lord for creating her as a woman, but rather denunciates the society for treating her unkindly and unequally. Rifaat's stand point with particular reference to Islam is therefore far from being rebellious. In his introduction to Rifaat's book, Denys Johnson-Davies makes an outstanding point when he mentions that "Rifaat's revolt, therefore, is merely against certain man-made interpretations and accretions that have grown up over the years and remain unquestioned by the majority of both women and men". Rifaat therefore seems to be taking an essentially feminist position by attempting to rewrite 'her-story' rather than 'history'. She is also able to draw clear divisions in her mind all the time between God's will and the will of men; without addressing the concept of atheism she vehemently criticizes the male traditional role in some Egyptian phallocentric societies.

Finally I would like to conclude by referring to Nawal El Saadawi, another pioneering Arab feminist who is best known for her provocative writings, often challenging the existing system and also the patriarchal power. Firdaus in Saadawi's *Woman at Point Zero* (1983) was subject to such brutality and inhumanity by certain individuals that detested with her life, she was eager to embrace death as life had no meaning left. On the other hand Rifaat's female protagonists choose to move on with life. The characters of both these authors lived within similar framework of culture and religion, and therefore, were subject to similar patriarchal subjection in various forms. These protagonists, after passing through existential vacuum, have ended up in searching for salvation. However, more particularly in Alifa Rifaat's stories, the protagonists have been the ones who realised their plight and inability in their daily routine and socially prevalent lifestyle and traditions, unlike Firdaus who was conned and betrayed several times. It is this fact of living within the accepted social norms and practices and then somehow not coming into alliance with it is what makes the protagonists of Rifaat's stories more contrasting and striking. It is as if they are uttering:

"Far away there in the sunshine are my highest aspirations. I may not reach them, but I can look up and see their beauty, believe in them, and try to follow where they lead." (Louisa May Alcott)

BIBLOGRAPHY

BOOKS

Bhasin, Kamala. *Understanding Gender*. New Delhi: Zubaan, 2000. Print.

Cooke, Mariam. *Tribal Modern: Branding New Nations in the Arab Gulf,* USA:University of California Press. 2013. Print.

El-Saadawi, Nawal. *The Nawal El-Saadawi Reader*. New York: St Martin's Press.1997. Print.

Menon, Nivedita. *Seeing Like a Feminist*. India: Zubaan, 2012. Print.

Mernissi, Fatima. *Beyond the Veil: Male-Female Dynamics in Modern Muslim Society*. Bloomington & Indianapolis: Indiana University Press, 1987. Print.

Moitra, Shefali. "The Sex/Gender System." in Feminist Thought: Androcenticism, Communication and Objectivity. New Delhi: MunshiramManoharlal Publisher, 2002, 6-29. Print.

Gul Ozyegin (Ed.), *Gender and Sexuality in Muslim Culture*, USA, Ashgate Publishing House, 1998, p. 282.

Moghadam, Valentine. *Modernizing Women: Gender & Social Change in the Middle East*. Boulder &London: Lynne Rienner, 1993. Print.

Mohanty, Chandra. Cartographies of Struggle: Third World Women and the Politics of Feminism. C. Mohanty, A. Russo & L. Torres (ed.). *Third World Women and the Politics of Feminism*. Bloomington & Indianapolis: Indiana University Press, 1991. Print.

Ozyegin, Gul (Ed.). *Gender and Sexuality in Muslim Culture*. USA: Ashgate Publishing House, 1998. Print.

Rifaat, Alifa. Denys Johnson-Davies (Translated) *Distant View of a Minaret and Other Stories.* Egypt: Heinemann (African Writers Series), 1983. Print.

Salti, Ramzi M. 'Feminism and Religion inAlifa Rifaat's Short Stories' in The International Fiction Review 18.2. USA: University of California, 1991. Print.

WEBSITES

http://www.bbc.co.uk/ accessed on 15 November, 2015.

http://www.feminist.com/ accessed on 22 November, 2015

Chapter 16

Representation of Women by Women novelist of Indian origin

MOUMITA BISWAS
Asst.Professor (English)
Maharani Kasiswari College
Ramkanta Bose Lane
Kolkata 700003

Feminism in India has often been called the "Feminism of compromise", for it is occasionally the feminism of women who collect big pay cheques by day but do not question their husbands. It is the feminism of educated Indian ladies who cope up privately with work-place harassment, but never see it as a systematic phenomenon to be fought. The Indian woman negotiates throughout her life with the patriarchal social setup which is characterized by three cults – the cult of 'true' womanhood, the cult of 'domesticity' and the cult of 'purity' – all these legitimize the victimization of women. The creative writings by the Indian women authors both within and outside the country bring before us a whole range of issues pertaining to the experience of Indian women in society. These authors speak out the tribulations and compromises of the Indian women and also some of their silent protest against the male dominated society and its inhuman laws. Their writings serve an explosion of suppressed desires and pent up feelings that have long been gathered and also plays significant role in making the society aware of the woman's needs and demands.

Anita Desai, in her novels, mainly explores the emotional world of women, revealing a rare imaginative awareness of various deeper forces at work and a profound understanding of feminine sensibility as well as psychology. She sets herself to voice the mute miseries and helplessness of millions of married women tormented by existentialist problems and predicaments. She is concerned with the problems faced by her protagonists. Her serious concern is the "journey within" and her central characters mostly being women. The recurring theme in her novels is the trauma of existence in a hostile, male dominated society that is conservative and taboo ridden. She portrays the inner conflicts of her characters and also underlines their individuality and quest for freedom. The feminine voice in the novels of Anita Desai expressed in her early work **Cry the Peacock** (1963) and her second novel **The voices in the city** (1965) articulates the yearnings of Indian women from affluent orthodox Hindu backgrounds who under the stress of the modern condition and in their mistaken seeking of forms of fulfillment not consonant with their upbringing, destroy themselves in insanity, despair or suicide. Desai seizes on the details of outward reality as images of landscape of the interior being of her women characters. Her feminist concern thus is modulated through a vivid realization of contemporary Indian social situations. The protagonists in Desai's **Where shall we go this summer?** (1975) Sita, is an Indian wife who revolts painfully but typically un- catastrophically against the everyday dreariness of her existence; in her next novel **Fire on the mountain** (1977) Desai presents Nanda, a lonely old lady, suffering from unfulfilling relationship and psychic disorders; she makes desperate attempt to escape from the harsh realities of life and her loneliness and takes refuge in her world of illusion. In fact, all the woman-characters of Desai cling to imagination as they fail to adapt to the real life situation or cope up with reality. This enhances the complexity in their character and turns them into 'neurotic females'; as N.R. Gopal points out:

> "Characters in novels of Mrs. A. Desai are generally neurotic females, highly sensitive but sequestered in a surrounding as a consequence of their failure or unwillingness to adjust with reality. They often differ in their opinion from others and embark on a long voyage of contemplation in order to find the meaning of their existence."

(Gopal: 7)

The best of Desai is **Clear light of day** (1980). The work traces an embittered woman's childhood and youth as she comes to understand her own femininity in her relationships with others. Desai's novels are never stridently 'Feminist' in the way much Western Feminist fictions are, but Desai unerringly represent the circumscribed and often claustrophobic life experiences of her women characters who attempt to reconcile illusions and reality, sometimes they prove successful but often ending up to suicide and death.

Arundhati Roy's prize winning novel **God of small things** (1999) has a woman character as the chief protagonist. The novel unfolds the subjective politics which has ordered the subjugation of women in a "man owned" world. Ammu, who is an educated middle class lady, having suffered in a dysfunctional marriage and having lived as a single woman in U.S.A., comes back to her native land to reunite with her children. The novel projects the multiple facets of Ammu as mother, dependant and divorced single woman struggling in a patriarchal society. The novelist has brilliantly projected the injustice inflicted upon women through the means of patriarchy, caste taboos and love-laws. The weight of Patriarchy ultimately breaks Ammu's spirits and causes her to meet an untimely death as she is rejected not only by her community but also her own family for daring to fall in love with an untouchable man and thereby violating the painful love laws prescribed by the phallic community. Roy's novel reminds us of the inevitable punishment that a woman gets whenever she goes against the social construct of ideal womanhood and bares to choose a life of freedom from norms and restrictions. The 'ideal' woman is not only assigned a social role that locks her within four walls but also ensures her subordinate 'Position' in the society, as Meitreyi Mukhopadhyay observes:

> "The inequality and subordination of women is an instrument or function of the social structure" (82).

Besides the society expects her to be cheerful and gay with her 'subordinate' position; Thus Roy's novel **"The god of small things"** exposes the hypocrisy and entrenched prejudices of traditional Indian society deepened in consciousness of class distinction and female inferiority.

Different from Anita Desai and Arundhati Roy, Shashi Despande sets herself the task of breaking what she describes in the title of a novel as **That long silence** (1988), which starts with the sentence:

> **"To achieve anything, you' ve got to be ruthless".**

Both this novel and its successor **The Binding Vine** (1993) focus on the life of a woman writer, Jaya, the protagonist of **That long silence** finds her voice only when her husband leaves her. Despande mostly shows how Jaya is trapped within her own inhibitions, her inability to free herself from the demand that she restricts herself to the 'Feminine' emotions. The patriarchy-generated myth that Jaya has internalized is:

> **"A woman can never be angry, she can only be neurotic, hysterical, frustrated".**

This points to Simone de Beauvoir's famous remark in her **The Second Sex** :

> **"One is not born but rather becomes woman ...... It is civilization as a whole that produces this creatures**

intermediate between male and eunuch, which is described as Feminine."

The subservience of the typical Indian married woman is represented through her husbands power of renaming her "Suhasini" on her marriage; her task is to abandon that name in favour of the name she was born with – 'Jaya', which means 'victory'.

In **The Binding Vine,** the sequel, Urmila, the protagonist is a woman grieving for the death of her infant daughter. Two projects reawaken her interests in life however. She discovers the diary and unpublished poems of Mira, her mother-in-law who had been repeatedly raped by her husband and had ultimately died in child-birth. Her second project is to win justice for Kalpana who lies throughout the story, silent and unconscious, the victim of a rape by her brother-in-law. Urmila is separated from Mira by her own relatively happy marriage and from Kalpana by history and social class, but the novel works to dismantle these distinctions. Unlike Jaya, Urmila is not permitted to emerge as victorious, but rather with a bleak sense that "the binding vine" – a phrase from one of Mira's poem – will continue to restrict woman under male power.

Despande's writings are like case studies of women full of reality. One can visualize with crystal clarity, the struggle and trauma they go through in their relationships pertaining to their surroundings, their society, their families, their children and especially with their men. In **The Long Silence**, Jaya's silence symbolizes the inability of most of the women in the world to express themselves as individuals. This silence gives her a way to search for identity. Despande is a moralist who teaches women to break the 'silence' and voice themselves, to fight for their liberation and get themselves free from existing existential predicament in a male dictated society. In one of her interview Shashi Despande states :

> **"If others see something feminist in my writings, I must say that is not consciously done. It is because the world for women is like that and I am mirroring the world."**

The Indian woman's experience on the foreign shores is projected by Bharati Mukherjee and Jhumpa Lahiri. Bharati Mukherjee's novels **Wife** and **Jasmine** chronicle the journeys of two young women to the U.S. for individual reasons, under dissimilar circumstances, both of them undergo torturous physical, mental and emotional agony affecting their whole being to such an extent that they are driven to violence. In Wife Mukherjee narrates the problems and humiliations that a married Indian woman encounters in a American milieu into which she has been transported after her marriage. In her feminist novel **Jasmine,** Mukherjee writes of an Indian woman Jyoti's transformation into an Asian-American who has pushed back her Indian past and Indian ethos. Jyoti reveals how a woman is compelled to change herself on the demand made by her surroundings.

Jhumpa Lahiri's work mainly deals with characters that are first and second generation members of the Indian Diaspora. Lahiri presents in her work woman's marginalisation in cultural context. The psychological trauma of Mrs. Das in the title story **The Interpreter of**

Maladies is attributed to Indian patriarchal notion of marriage. Her individuality is forcefully taken away by the dominant notion of marriage in patriarchal society. Her emotions are given no importance, even by her family, to whom the only thing that matters is her marriage. But even after marriage nothing changes for her, in fact, the emotional negligence continues – she suffers the negligence of her husband who prefers to keep himself busy in work. However, she tries to assert her female individuality: first by entering into sexual relationship with her husband's male friend and second by retracting from the sexual relationship with Dev to save from reducing herself merely to a sexual object. The first generation immigrant women in Jhumpa Lahiri's work are often subjected to patriarchal marginalisation. Ashima in **The Namesake** and Ruma's mother in **Unaccustomed Earth** are first generation immigrants who exemplify woman's conformist attitude to the patriarchy.

Thus the study reveals the responsibility shouldered by the women writers of Indian origin to project the predicament of women in a male dominant society. Their writings mark their restless effort to voice the pathos, the humility and the subjugated existence of women in our society. The variety of subjects handled by these writers not only gives weightage to their writings but also plays an indispensable role in constructing awareness for the modern women all over the globe. Although some of the writers have not claimed their attachment to any feminist movement yet their inner spirit and feelings indicate clearly their concern for the welfare of the women of our society.

REFERENCES

1. Anita Desai, <u>Cry, The Peacock</u>, Delhi: Orient Paperback, 1980.
2. Anita Desai, <u>Voices in the city</u>, Delhi: Orient Paperback, 1980.
3. Despande Sashi, <u>The Long Silence</u>: 1988 (New Delhi Penguin India Ltd.).
4. Gopal N.R. <u>A Critical Study of the Novels of Anita Desai</u> (Atlantis publishers and Distributors).
5. Mukherjee Bharati, <u>Wife</u>, (New Delhi Penguin Books, 1990).
6. Mukherjee Bharati, <u>Jasmine</u>, New York Groove Press.
7. Mukhopadhyay Meitreyi <u>Indian Women: Change and Challenges in the International Decade</u> (1975-85, Bombay Popular Prakashan, 1985)
8. Roy Arundhati, <u>The God of Small Things</u> (New Delhi: Indian Ink, 1997).

Chapter 17

Manusamhita: A Feminist Approach

ARPITA CHAKRABORTY
Assistant Teacher
Gangnapur High School (Girls)
Gangnapur, Dhantala, Nadia

The *Manusaṃhitā* is a very popular and much discussed book in the Indian society and the history of literature. This book consists of twelve chapters. It is famous as "*Dharmaśāstras*", the religious book. The Śrautasūtra, the *Gṛjhyasūtra,* the *Manusaṃhitā*, the *Yājñabalkyasaṃhitā*, the *Mahābhārata* which were composed after Veda, are included in the "*smṛtiśāstra*". Later on the Vedic age, according to the real meaning of the Vedic mantras, the sacrificial rites became very hard. So there arises the necessity of the new explanation of "dharma". In that time charity, vows etc. were described as the new definition of "*Dharma*" in the "*purāṇa*" literature. And which scripture was composed as a symbol of the "dharma", narrated in "*purāṇas*" may be called "*Dharmaśāstras*". Such "*Dharmaśāstras*" was known as "*smṛtiśāstra*". Among the compositors of this "*smṛtiśāstras*" the great Manu has been considered the best. His composition is known as the "*Manusaṃhitā*".

The sage Bhṛgu had learned the whole *"Manusaṃhitā"* from *Maharsi* Manu. The respected Manu had declared to the other great sages that only the sage Bhṛgu deserved to tell this holy book thoroughly. In this books many times "Manu is saying" was revealed by "manur āha", "manur abrabīt", "manur anu śāsanam" etc. So there is no disagreement that the great sage Manu was the main compositor of the *Manusaṃhitā,* although it was told by the sage Bhṛgu.

We get the name of Manu in ancient age of Veda. It proves the ancientness of Manu. It was imagined that in ancient age the world was divided by seven islands. There lived seven races in those seven islands. Those were the main races. The earlier father of every main race was Manu. So there were the existences of seven Manus. They were S̲v̲ā̲y̲a̲ṃ̲b̲h̲u̲b̲a̲, S̲v̲ā̲r̲o̲c̲i̲ṣ̲a̲, A̲u̲t̲t̲a̲m̲i̲, T̲ā̲m̲a̲s̲a̲, R̲a̲i̲b̲a̲t̲a̲, C̲ā̲k̲ṣ̲u̲ṣ̲a̲ and V̲a̲i̲v̲a̲s̲v̲a̲t̲a̲. Among them V̲a̲i̲v̲a̲s̲v̲a̲t̲a̲ ̲M̲a̲n̲u̲ was considered as the earlier father of the Ā̲r̲y̲a̲. In the opinion of Shree Hirendranath Dutta those Manus were not the name of an individual person – "it is the designation of an office".

To point out the actual time of composition of the *Manusaṃhitā* is very difficult. P.V.Kane exposed his opinion about the relation between the *Mahābhārata* and the *Manusaṃhitā* by discussing thoroughly the views of the eastern and the western scholars. According to the view of P.V.Kane the composition of the *Mahābhārata*, in which form we get it now, was completed after the *Manusaṃhitā*, which is found now. About the time of composition of the *Manusaṃhitā* he said, "My own position is that the original Manusmriti in verse had certain additions made in order to bring it in a line with the change in the general attitude of people on several points such as those of flash-eating, *niyoga*, etc. But all these additions must have been made long before the 3rd century A.D. as the quotations from Brihaspati and others show." By discussing all opinions Bühler came to this view that the *Manusaṃhitā* was composed in any time from the 2nd century B.C. to the 2nd century A.D.

Though the *Manusaṃhitā* was composed supporting on the Vedic thoughts, but when this book was composed, it told more new points which were proper for that age and society. There were discussed about the source of the world, *"saṃskāra vidhi"*, regulations of marriage, the duties of the king and citizens, the rituals of Hindus in this holy book. The right and the dignity of the women were much discussed in this religious book. Although Manu did not admit the liberation of women in all fields but by discussing his all verses we come to understand that he was for the feminism.

It is said clearly in third chapter of the *Manusaṃhitā* that, in which family women are respected, God is also satisfied there. But where women are neglected, all sacrifices for God become fruitless:-

> *Pitṛbhir bhrātṛbhiś caitāḥ patibhir debarais tathā/*
> *Pūjyā bhūṣayitavyāś ca bahukalyānam īpsubhiḥ//*
> *Yatra nāryyas tu pūjyante ramante tatra devatāḥ/*
> *Yatraitās tu na pūjyante sarvās tatrāfalāḥ kriyāḥ//*

The great sage Manu said that *dharma, artha*, and *karma* of family life is depended on wives. For this, husband should respect their own wife. According to *Maharsi* Manu, in which family women are become sad express deep grief, such families will ruined soon. In the other hand, where women are happy, they gain property.

> *Śocanti jāmayo yatra binaśyanty āśu tat kulam/*
> *Na śocanti tu yatraitā barddhate tat dhi sarvadā//*

So, according to *Maharsi* Manu, who wants to improve in life, he should try to happy his wife.

Again Manu said that, women are the beauty of the home. They are very lucky for increasing their family by producing child. So there are no difference between "Śree" and "Stree". Wives are the main helpers to produce children, to look after them, to serve guests etc. from these sayings we come to know clearly that the great sage Manu did not neglect the women. Rather he respected them.

Great Manu said that it is our duty to protect the women from all adultery. He said that women should be protected by their father in their unmarried period, by their husbands in youth and by sons in their old age.

> *Pitā rakṣati kaumāre bhartā rakṣati yauvane/*
> *Rakṣati sthavire putrā na strī svatantryam arhati//*

At any cost women do not deserve independence. when she lives under whom, he must protect her. Though, according to Medhātithi, the renowned explainer of the *Manusaṃhitā*, all kinds of independences of women were not prohibited by Manu in this verse. But it is wanted to make understand by Manu that they are not able to rescue themselves if they are given freedom: "...... *yadā yadā adhinā tadā tadā tenābashyaṃ rakṣitabyā.........tathā darshitaṃ* mānabe- sarve ete sarvadā tat saṃrakṣanaṃ kuryuh........

"nanu cehāpi padyate 'na stree svātantram arhatiti'" ucyate. Nāneba sarvakriyābisayam svātantryam bidhiyate, kim tarhi, nāsvatantrā' nyam naskā svātmasamraksanāya pra bhabati saktibikaltvāt……." In different verse the great Manu said that women are not protected if they are imprisoned in home by forced. Those women who can rescue themselves from all dangers, are protected from all difficulties

Araksitā grhe ruddhāḥ purusair āptakāribhiḥ/
Ātmānm ātmanā yās tu rakṣeyus tāḥ su rakṣitāḥ//

It is cleared that the respected Manu was for the self-defense of women.

The great sage Manu always wanted to see that husbands are devoted to their wives.

Ṛtu kālābhigāmī syāsvadānirataḥ sadā/

He advised women that they also should be devoted to their husbands. In that age of Manu, There was no lack of characterless women in society. Some men were misguided by the attraction of women's beauty.

Svabhāva eṣa nārīṇām iha dūṣaṇam/
Ato' rthān na pra mādyanti pramadāsu bipaścitaḥ//

In this world women distract men by sexual apeal. This is not discredit of women. Everybody is addicted by sex, passion, anger etc. women can guide all educated or uneducated guys to the right or wrong path by their own wishes.

Abidvāṃsaṃ alaṃ loke bidvāṃsaṃ api vā punaḥ/
Pramadā hy utpathaṃ netuṃ kāmakrodhabaśānugam//

The great Manu had ordered to punish for adultery for both of men and women. There are some women who give up their husbands for the pride of the prosperity of their father's house or for the beauty of herself. Manu, the social welfare worker, indicated that, those women should be bitten by dogs in the public place

Bhartāraṃ laṅghayet yā tu stri jñāti-guṇa-darpitā/
Tāṃ śvabhiḥ khādayed rājā saṃ sthāne bahusaṃ sthite//

And that man, with whom the women had behaved adultery, is sentenced to death by lying on the burning-iron-sticks and the burning wood also will be thrown on him till his death.

Pumāṃsaṃ dāhayet pāpaṃ śayane tapta āyase /
Abhy ādadhyuś ca kāṭhāni tatra dahyeta pāpakṛt//

He also ordered that the women who committed adultery and were enjoyed by many persons, were called "bratya nari". There was hard punishment for such women. Marriage is the main objective of women. Even marriage is their "upanayan". To serve husband after marriage is the abode [15] like Guru's home. To marry is very necessary for women. If the wife is faithful, her husband's duty is to support her best. By this God is also pleased.

15

Devadattāṃ patir bhāryāṃ vindate necchayātmanaḥ/
Tāṃ sādhvīṃ bibhṛyāt nityaṃ devānāṃ priyam ācaran//

It is also said by Manu that although marriage is the main necessity in women's life, but it is the duty of her parents to give her marriage with a proper and pretty groom.

Utkṛistāyābhirūpāya varāya sadṛśāya ca/

Maharsi Manu said that, girls will stay at their father's home up to their death, yet they will not be given to an unfit groom. From these sayings, we come to know that *Maharsi* Manu was very respectful about women's dignity. It is also indicated by *Maharsi* Manu that if parents do not make their daughter married within selected period, then she can select her groom herself. It is not any type of sin. In this case Manu is familiar to us as a broad minded man.

Especially *Maharsi* Manu had a high thinking about women. There are many examples about this in the Manusaṃhitā. But again we get some verses where he reprehended the women. Such as, he had called the women as "puṃścalī", because she tempts by sexual intercourse with the men as soon as she looks at him. It is seen that there is impatience of the women in religious activities. The women become unsatisfied to their husbands in spite of their well looking after. Women's habits are to sleep very much, to stay being workless, to decorate herself with ornaments, sex-urge, hot-temper, mean nature, to addict to a vile etc. according to "śastra" there are no right of women to chant of Vedic mantras. They are harassed by wicked persons because they have no patience and wisdom and strength etc. their character and affections are also not fixed.

By discussion of the other verses of the Manusaṃhitā, composed about women, these condemnatory speeches are certainly inconsistent. A few critics have tried to prove Manu's displeased attitude about women by these inconsistent speeches. They forget that the great Manu highly praised the women in many verses of this book. It has been said in the second chapter of this book that, anybody must the place and give space for women for her honor.

Cakriṇo daśamisthasya rogiṇo bhāriṇaḥ striyāḥ/
Snātakasya ca rājñaś ca panthā deyo barasya ca//

even the equal rights of the male female are indicated in ninth chapter of the *Manusaṃhitā* –

Yathaibātmā tathā putraḥ putreṇa duhitā samā/

It is not exaggerated that which condemnatory verses about the women Manu had composed, these are for some characterless women who are seen in all countries and in all times. So who attempt to apply these censure remarks for all kinds of women, they give us the sign of foolishness. Although Shree Hirendranath Dutta thinks that these are really reprehension of women, which are truly opposite of previous sayings. *Makṣikā braṇamicchanti*: flies search the wounded places of animal body, later on just like someone who thought himself as a social welfare worker and also envied the women, had composed these condemnatory verses about the women and added them in the Manusaṃhitā. Shree Hirendranath Dutta considers them as "*prakṣipta*", the interpolated.

We can reach to the decision from the *Manusaṃhitā* that the women were respected and honored in that time. The great sage Manu tried to establish the right and the dignity of women. At present age we discuss and make movements about the dignity and right of the women. But there was no real honor of women anywhere of the society. They are neglected and ignored everywhere. Even now rape, killing and oppressing the wife etc. are happened. Though in ancient age the great sage Manu thought about the feminism, yet we cannot able to fulfill his purpose even now. When we can make the society where the dignity and right of the women will be well established, we will be to show respect *Maharsi* Manu.

BIBLIOGRAPHY

Bhattacharya, Dr. Hemanta.*kālidas o bhavabhutir sāhitye nāricaritra: Kolkata,* Sanskrit book dipo, 2003.

Jha, Ganganath. *Manusmrti Medhātithiracita Manubhāsya sametā (vol. 1, 2);* Delhi, Primal publications

Saptatirtha, Shree Bhutnath. *Manusmṛti Medhātithibhāsya (vol.1, 2, 3)*; Kolkata, sanskrit college: 1361(beng).

Shastri, Acharya Jagadishlala. *Manusmrti* (1st ed); Delhi, Motilal varanasidas, 1983.

Vandyopadhyaya, Manabendu. *Manusamhitā; Kolkata,* Sanskrit pustak bhandar, 2012.

Dutta, shree Hirendranath, *Manur barnashramdharma,*

Chapter 18

The Tragic Trio:
Interpreting Amba, Madri and Uttara
from a Feminist Point of View

DEBALINA ROYCHOWDHURY
M.A., M.Phil, English
Senior Lecturer, In charge of ED Cell
Elitte Institute of Engineering & Management

Mahabharata, the greatest epic can be considered as a heritage of India. It imbibes the saga of human struggle, conflict of ethics and many more. As it popularly goes that, 'anything that is not in Mahabharata does not exist anywhere in the world'. True it is that we can find the vivid range of human culture and conflict.

The feminine struggle, identity crisis and establishment of self-respect strongly echo throughout the epic. The women characters of the epic are prominent in bravery and courage; be that Ganga or Satyavati, Gandhari or Kunti, Draupadi or Subhadra – all are bright and dazzling in their own struggle and 'self' establishment. The female characters of Mahabharat are brilliant in their royal nature, beauty and impetus. Each of them is distinct and indomitable. Among all other women, three rarely explored ones are Amba, Madri and Uttara.

Amba, the princess of Kashi first strikes a different note of struggle in the epic. Betrothed to Salvaraj, she was waiting her groom in the Swayambar with her sisters Ambika and Ambalika. Despite getting married all the three sisters were abducted by Mahamati Bhisma. Bhisma's attack could not be resisted by other kings of the 'Sabha' and the nearly aged hero carried away the three princesses to Hastinapur to get married to Bichitrabirya. The three princesses kept silence.

On the way, Bhisma encountered an attack by Salvaraj which was immediately turned down by the former. But Amba retained her silence even there which is stunning; she did not confess about her affair at that juncture. Naturally the question arises - why? What made Amba, betrothed to Salvaraj, willing and wishing to marry him, remain quiet?

It may be considered that Amba developed an admiration for the Kurusreshth Bhishma. When Kashi Swayambarsabha was attacked by Gangaputra, she probably developed an intense appreciation for the valiant, worthy Bhishma. Amba was fascinated with the Ksatriya style of abducting the princess and grandeur of fight. Thus she did not express her feeling for Salvaraj in front of Bhishma. Perhaps this was the reason why she retained her silence even when Salvaraj attacked and lost the war with Devabrat.

This becomes more confirmed by her time of confession. She admitted the fact when she discovered that all the three spinster sisters were to be married with Bichitrabirya and not Bhishma. Probably then, Amba decided to return to Salvaraj and confessed the truth. This was accepted by Bhishma with full esteem and she was sent back to her betrothed lover. There again Amba was hindered by her lover and denied. Salva said that she had been abducted by someone and this retarded him to marry her. Amba, at this point, was treated as a commodity and abnegated by her fiance. Amba, then, as lore say, went back to Bhishma and asked him to marry her. But *Mahabharata* never says this.

According to the great epic, Amba having enough self-respect never went to Bhishma directly but reared up a deep hatred and grudge for him. This malice was an outcome of thwarted passion and attraction. Thus Amba's anger shifted towards Bhishma – not for Kashiraj who gave a swayambar of a betrothed girl or even not for Salvaraj who rejected his fiancé only for a baseless pride. This unreasonably acute antipathy came from nothing but barred attraction and suppressed passion. But, unlike legends, she never came back to Bhishma and asked him to marry due to her staunch self respect,

> "*Na cha*
> *sakyanggantangtatrabaroshahyam*".

Then she started to plot his devastation. She requested her grandfather Srinjay Hotrovan to fight against Bhishma. Hotrovam appealed to his friend Parashuram to teach Bhishma, his student a lesson. Unwillingly Parashuram summoned this Kurusreshth for a war. This war is treated as an exceptional one where a student triumphs over his adept teacher, Parashuram. This made the Acharya elated to see the expertise of his student and blessed him from the core of his heart.

Amba was left with only the second and protracted way of avenging her revilement that was her 'Tapasya'. She, then, devoted the rest of the life in her 'sadhana' and never returned in a normal life. Mahabharata says that Bhishma appointed some officials to keep an eye on this exasperated 'mystery' lady who focused only on the way to take revenge on Bhishma. This is again striking because what what made Bhishma appoint spies to look on her? And if he would not have sworn for his lifelong bachelorship, would he not marry Amba? There is a deep laden strain that Bhishma developed an affection for Amba.

Later on rebirth of Amba was possible for her grave 'Tapasya' at Drupad's dwelling as Shikhandi, the Bramhastra against Bhishma. There are other tales and lore regarding Shikhandi that Shikhandi was born as a woman and he exchanged his genitals with a 'Yaksa' for the sake of avenging. Shikhandi, then arrives in the Kurukshetra, deeply inclined to confront with 'Gangaputra'.

According to Srikrishna's scheme Shikhandi accompanied Arjuna to pull down the curtain of Bhishma's life. Bhishma the pioneer of the epic leaves his arms as he confronts Shikhandi in the war field, he considered Shikhandi as a woman and as a true 'kshatriya' and he denounced his weapon and invited the arrows of Arjuna. The wearied and valiant soldier took his 'Sarasajya'. He stayed in the war front but accepted his last defeat that too for the reason, - Amba. An exceptional love-hate relationship. The struggle and loneliness of Amba plays a trenchant note in the epic. A woman driven by passion unknown to her and derided by revenge. Fate leaves her incomplete in both the two lives.

Madri was the sister of Saalvaraaj and the princess of Madra. She was popular for her ecstatic beauty and virtues. Bhishma went to her brother Saalva with the proposal for Paandu and Madri's marriage. For this Bhishma gave the latter lots of gold, elephants, horses and other precious gifts according to their family custom. Ultimately Saalva let her go with the great Gangaputra for her marriage. Madri was the second wife of Paandu. The king was first married to Kunti who had a superior personality than her. The impetus, the brightness, the prowess of Kunti surmised that of Madri. She surely felt inferior which she confessed later. The only feature that is highlighted in her is her beauty. Probably this poignantly and tragically brings forth the massive difference.

After the marriage Paandu went out for invasion. At his successful return he decided to go to the Tapovan of Himavat. We know that, Paandu killed a large deer while it was copulating. The large male deer was struck by the five arrows. It fell down and wept bitterly like that of a man. The legend says that it was not a deer at all, it was Rishi Kindam with a great ascetic merit. The deer cursed Paandu that he will immediately meet his end when he will get united with his wife. If we really go deep into the story, does it satisfy our belief? I have found Mahabharata to be the most scientific and logical epic; besides wherever something is hidden or that which is not described vividly for any reason (social or political) is presented under a garb of an exaggerated story. The story heightens symbolically but apparently it conceals the real facts. The dying deer's curse again puts forth our doubt to the same point. The doubt strikes at the particular point and that is the in the marital relationship of the great king Paandu.

I felt that the sudden 'Tapovan trip' of Paandu and his two wives is really striking. Leaving the two wives, just a month after his second marriage Paandu decided to go for the conquest. And just after returning he started for

Tapovan. Naturally the question arises why? Was it only for the sake of acquiring '*Punya*'? The connecter seems weak. This can be supported by Kunti's statement which I would discuss later.

Anyway, after being cursed, Paandu made a journey to reach paradise during he practiced celibacy and was hindered by the Rishis and Sidhdhas as he was without an heir. Thus he had to return unfulfilled. The king then discussed with Kunti and requested her to 'raise offspring at a time of distress.' He mentioned total six kinds of sons that were told by the religious institutes and six other kinds in addendum. The conversation between them was in private where Madri was not present. The absence of Madri in this crucial discussion leads to a question that where does she stand? She was a mere beautiful and appealing wife than a one whom he could depend upon. But Kunti plays a vital role of a guardian or guide.

Kunti then summoned the three potent Gods and received three powerful sons after getting spiritually united with them. The first son Yudhistira was born before Gandhari gave birth to her first son. The three sons were born due to the repeated request of Paandu. Madri privately approached Paandu and stated about her misery. If we follow her speech, some striking points come forth. Madri felt the fact that she was overshadowed by Kunti and Paandu was prejudiced to her. If this be right then Kunti's speech later when Paandu dies focuses that Madri was lucky that Paandu shared the loved moments with her. If we consider both the view then what kind of importance did Madri receive? Or even similar question stands for Kunti. Again, Madri also points out that she was superior to Kunti by birth. The pain and inferiority plays a mild symphony through this character. She then urges Paandu to request Kunti to help her in becoming mother. Even she addresses her to be her 'rival' and thus feeling shy to approach her directly. This type of comment or mentality did not flicker in Kunti as far as the great epic is concerned. It seemed to me that the king became greedy for more descendants and pressurized Kunti for the expansion of his race, to which Kunti denied telling him that a fourth attempt would make her "*Swairini*" (heanton)Paandu then said to her.

"Therefore, O blameless one, rescue this Madri as by a raft (by granting her the means of obtaining offspring), and achieve thou imperishable fame by making her a mother of children."

Probably Kunti was tired of the process and readily yielded. Why did Madri call the Ashwins and not any other potential Gods? Two possible reasons are there according to my view.

First, as she knew that she can use the means once only, she thought to have twin babies. This sharply points at her inferiority complex that played deep in her mind. She did not want to stay too much inferior to Kunti. So she called the Ashwins to get two children. Secondly, VedVyas wanted to maintain the discrimination between the two wives of Paandu, in terms of greatness. Thus, Surya, Dharma, Pavan, Indra and then Ashwins are bit mismatch.

Being second wife does not always mean soothing life. Madri though higher in status could never reach the height of Kunti, who was more like a 'Godmother' to the family. She remained more like an object of desire than anything else. This is strongly specified at the death of Paandu. He and his two wives stayed in the midst of the forest with their five handsome sons. It happened thus on a day of spring, when the nature was in her peak of beauty Paandu felt his desire blowing mildly. He saw Madri in her translucent attire which ignited and overpowered him at the moment. He seized Madri against her will and embraced her. The hapless wife tried to resist the king and failed. If we analyse the woman's condition we can feel her misery prominently. She, despite loving Paandu and devoid of conjugal pleasure helplessly hinders her loved one who forcefully begets her. Well aware of the consequence, the woman becomes a mere puppet in the hands of desire and blame. She does not allure Paandu but becomes the pathetic reason for his death. Kunti reaches the place hearing her cries and blames her with sobs. We get a picture of Kunti there as a woman who nearly mothered her husband and cared him. She also says:

"Dhanyatvamasi Bahleekimattobhagyataratatha
Drsavatyasiyadvaktramprahrshtasyamahipateh"

(Adi 124, 21)

This means,

> 'O princess of Valhika, more fortunate
> than me, thou art really to be envied, for
> thou hast seen the face of our lord suffused
> with gladness and joy.'

Kunti here was referring to the ecstasy of sexual climax that lingered in the dead face. If we delve the depths of the speech, Paandu again can be proved as a man either impotent or having some disorder because he had left his first wife deprived of the pleasure though she accompanied him even before the curse fell.

Listening to the wish of Kunti of following Paandu, Madri desisted her with reverence and sought her permission to go with the King. She admits that she even would not be able to perform the role of a true mother as Kunti will be. Leaving the two babies in Kunti's (her rival's) refuge she becomes a Sati.

This honesty of confessing in Madri is highly worth praise that had the guts to express Kunti as her rival and admit her as a superior at the same time. Madri thus remain as a tragic melody in the pages of Mahabharata.

Uttara is the third of the trio, she is the princess of Virat. She is introduced in the Agyatvas of the Pandavas. When Kauravas attacked Virat Kingdom, Prince Uttar was about to go to fight with the Kauravas, it was at the verge of completion of their *Agyatavas*. Draupadi suggested her to ask Vrihannala to accompany to him. Uttara rushes to convince him Arjun and Uttara the Epic writer has used the typical theorem of that of a hero & heroine of a hint of adoration, an exalted love is mildly present in the penpicture of Uttara-Arjuna relationship. A hero worship of admiration for the hero like personality is revealed. A hint of closeness is present in between the Guru and the student. Later, when the king of Virat offered Uttara's suit for Arjuna revealed, deals it with tremendous maturity. As students belong to the status of ward, Arjuna finds his son suitable for Uttara. The way Arjun addresses Uttara, is bit different than that of a teacher. This is a strange but realistic feeling that prevails. Humans are of variety and outré is their feelings. All the feeling cannot be actually named or expressed. A different sterling and sweat adoration grew between the teachers and the student.

Realising the adoration of the girl Arjun handed it in a mature way, when Viratraj offered him to marry his daughter Arjun considering the teacher student liaison offers her the suit for his son Abhimanyu, saying that a student is like a ward to a teacher.

Vyasa draws a pen picture of Uttara as an exuberant girl demanding clothes from Kauravas to her teacher who goes for a war; it is obvious that she is a jovial innocent pampered girl surely having lots of dream for her married life. Abhimanyu is seen to have been more dedicated towards the epical war which was at near future than his beautiful wife. The very next morning the little Arjun is seen to participate in the political discussion with his kinsmen. The marriage tenure is of merely six months. Abhimanyu is killed heinously by the seven members of the Kauravs.

Uttara at time was pregnant. The pampered innocent lovely princess' Pain can be traced. A minimal married life when Abhimanyu dies, the reference of Uttara is strikingly less. She is more highlighted not for her loss of husband but for her pregnancy; this indicates the socio-political scenario gaining more importance than humanity. The death of the husband suddenly presents Uttara as a mature balanced lady. The Brahmaslir charged by Aswathama. Krishna saved life of the newborn. The baby was a six month born. Now the lady is known for premature delivery. The pain of a bereaved wife merges with the return pain of a bereaved mother. She pleads to Krishna

"Bahabaaasanmanoratha"
                                   - (lots of dream I have for this son)

She said she did not end her life even after Abhimanyu died because of her son. Now when he is born dead, Krishna has to save him. The posthumous child was born hinted as still born, but saved by Krishna and the pain of the mother is relieved.

May be she does not take a big area in the Epic nor any grandiloquence she holds like Kunti or Draupadi, but strikes a trenchant tune of pain especially as she undergoes transformation from sweetness to realism, joviality to graveness, immaturity to sensibility.

These three characters though less discussed are brightly present in the epic. The tragic pattern in the three women is of isolation and loneliness and deprivation and the way the individual faced. Unlike the protagonists like Kunti, Draupadi, they are characters of lesser importance, especially Madri and Uttara. They fall under the genre of eternal feminine crisis and vulnerability in the world of men. The constant struggle with the social rituals, norms and ethics nearly congealed there way of life; still the struggle did never cease. Though they received less importance but their ceaseless conflict portrays them as unique in the tragic genre. Amba, the eternal rebel, Madri, the inferior identity and Uttara, the upright young mother remain glorious in their individuality.